On Time Delivery

On Time Delivery

the dog team mail carriers

William S. Schneider

University of Alaska Press
Fairbanks

University of Alaska Press
P.O. Box 756240
Fairbanks, AK 99775-6240

ISBN 978-1-60223-167-2 (paperback); 978-1-60223-168-9 (e-book)

Library of Congress Cataloging-in-Publication Data

Schneider, William.
 On time delivery : the dog team mail carriers / William Schneider.
    p. cm.
 Includes bibliographical references and index.
 ISBN 978-1-60223-167-2 (pbk. : alk. paper)—ISBN 978-1-60223-168-9 (ebook)
 1. Dogsled mail—Alaska—History. 2. Letter carriers—Alaska—Biography.
 3. Mushers—Alaska—Biography. 4. Alaska—Biography. 5. Frontier and pioneer
 life—Alaska. 6. Community life—Alaska—History. 7. Alaska—History, Local.
 8. Alaska—Social life and customs. I. Title.
 HE6376.A1A47 2012
 383'.143—dc23   2011033431

Cover and text design by Paula Elmes, Imagecraft Publications & Design
Cover illustrations: Maurice O'Leary on the mail trail over Eagle Summit, UAF
Rasmuson Library Archives, 2011-0025-0004; Alaska Road Commission map, 1914.

This publication was printed on acid-free paper that meets the minimum
requirements for ANSI / NISO Z39.48–1992 (R2002) (Permanence of Paper for
Printed Library Materials).

Printed on recycled paper in the United States

Remembering

Yukon

Lincoln

Rooster

Yankee

Dempsey

Ginger

All Heroes of the Trail

Contents

Introduction

The Iditarod and Yukon Quest sled dog races are faint but important reminders of a period in Alaska history when over-land trails provided transport and communication over much of the vast Interior. Dog team mail carriers, responsible for regular scheduled delivery of mail and freight regardless of weather and trail conditions, made up the backbone of this system. Today, planes provide point-to-point travel over vast stretches that once supported a different way of life, a life more dependent on the land. This book sets out to tell that story.

While the modern long-distance sled dog racers remind us of the old trails, they also provide a striking contrast to the dog team mail carriers. The racers are out for speed. They carry a minimum of weight, travel mostly over trails broken out by snow machines, and run sleek, fast dogs: their goal is to beat the competition. This is quite different from the historic mail carrier days when each dog driver was a human link in a chain of communication that moved the mail across the North. The goal of each mail carrier was to be ready to pick up the mail from one musher and deliver it on time and safely down the trail to the next waiting mail carrier. While the mail carriers' dogs were stout and tough, hardened to pulling big loads over rough trails, the modern race dogs are lean, bred to run fast, and trained to run long distances.

The modern dog racers travel through large stretches of wilderness and unsettled country, blinding us to the history of activity and settlement along those same trails. The trails once supported travel through the country on land rather than by air, the predominant mode of travel today. In the mail carriers' day, the trails were the connecting link for mail, people, and the latest news that traveled from camp to camp, roadhouse to roadhouse.

Many young people in rural Alaska grow up today with little understanding of the land their grandparents knew and used, the villages and camps that were essential to their lives. The modern dog team racers keep some of the trails open, but their rest stops are too short, their eyes too directed on the finish line, and there are too few old-timers left to take them back in time with the stories of life in the country. I hope this book will take us down that trail.

Before the gold rushes, there was little need for mail service in interior Alaska. The population was largely illiterate, save the few traders serving the Native population of Indians who lived in small, widely dispersed bands. The turn of the nineteenth and beginning of the twentieth century, however, brought prospectors and entrepreneurs streaming into interior Alaska in search of gold. The mail was their lifeline back home to relatives, loved ones, and business partners. They expected and demanded the mail service they had always enjoyed, and they complained when the mail was delayed. As a group, they were more literate than any generation before them, and the trails were the link that made winter mail delivery possible.

Unraveling the story of dog team mail carriers has been a personal adventure, and so I have tried to recognize and describe some of the usual and unusual archival sources that have brought this story to light for me as well as highlighting some of the people who shared their stories with me. I have steered clear of many of the sensational stories of overcoming extreme conditions of weather and trail. Many of those have already been told, and that's not the way the mail carriers saw their work. The carriers, their families, and the communities they served did not see the history of dog team mail carriers as a sensational story but as part of their everyday lives. That's not to say that the job wasn't dangerous by any standard. Probably Hudson Stuck, the Episcopal churchman who traveled many of the trails, provided the most sobering but balanced perspective on winter travel:

> The old-timers in Alaska have a saying that "travelling at 50 degrees below is all right as long as it's all right." If

there be a good trail, if there be convenient stopping places,
if nothing goes wrong. . . . (Stuck 2005[1914]:14)

RECONSTRUCTING A WAY OF LIFE

The last dog team mail carrier, Chester Noongwook, drove his dogs
between Savoonga and Gambell on St. Lawrence Island in January 1963
(Simpson 1996:25), two years after President Kennedy unveiled his plan
for a manned lunar landing and six years before Neil Armstrong set foot
on the moon. Although airplanes had replaced dog teams on most routes
in interior Alaska by the mid-1940s, Noongwook's run officially marked
the end of an era. Now, with the exception of Noongwook, I don't believe
any of the dog team mail carriers are still living. Fortunately, there are
people who remember, from their childhoods, the last of the men who
ran the mail, those who broke trail for miles on snowshoes after heavy
snow, the fishermen who provided food for the dogs, and the system of
roadhouses that sheltered them along the way. The passing of that way
of life signaled a fundamental change in winter travel and the connections
between communities.

Dog teams and horses carried mail in interior Alaska from the late 1890s
until the 1940s. The system of trails led from year-round ice-free ports on
the coast far into the Interior where gold was discovered and where there
was a population of prospectors. For Native people of interior Alaska, the
new centers of commerce offered opportunities for employment. The magazines and newspapers brought by the mail exposed many Natives to a world
apart from the subsistence round that sustained their way of life. Today, the
story of the men who carried the mail, the families who supported them,
and the knowledge of the very trails they traveled on are but dim recollections. Their accounts are a reminder that we have captured only the tail end
of this important era. Fortunately, those accounts allow us to reconstruct
some of the connections between people living in camps, roadhouses, and
communities before aviation changed transportation in Alaska forever. My
most important living links back to this period in history have been people
like Paul Esai, who broke trail for Charlie Shade, and Todd Kozevnikoff,
Sally Hudson, and George O'Leary, who as kids and young adults traveled
with the mail carriers at the end of the dog team mail era. This work is written as much as possible in their words, but, for older records, I turned to
archives in Fairbanks, Whitehorse, and Washington, D.C.

SCOPE OF THIS WORK

The story of dog team mail for all of Alaska is beyond the scope of this work. The area under consideration here extends from McGrath on the west, Allakaket and Alatna to the north, Dawson on the east, and Valdez to the south.

There are several reasons for limiting this research. Most of the major gold strikes occurred in the Interior, within the area covered by this work. The major exceptions are Nome and Juneau, but even Nome in winter had to be reached from the interior trail system, and the trunk and limbs of that system extended through the country described here.

The second reason for choosing the Interior is personal. I set out not only to document the dog team mail carrier history of routes, but also to learn about the individuals who carried the mail. It would be easy to see the mail service as a white man's enterprise. Many of the earliest carriers were white, but the story of dog team mail service is in many respects also a Native story. Many of the carriers were Native in the forty years of dog team mail carriers serving the Interior, from the gold rushes in the early 1900s to the establishment of scheduled airplane service in the 1940s. Most mail carriers, Native or white, were married to Native women, and there are several examples of children of mixed marriage taking over the mail run from their white fathers. All the carriers were dependent on bales of dried fish to feed their dogs on the trail, and these were largely supplied by Native fishermen. Their sleds, clothing, and methods of care for the dogs largely followed Native tradition and design.

The mail carrier enjoyed a high-status, well-paying position that cut across ethnic lines. However, the prevailing historical accounts of this time indicate widespread discrimination toward Natives in Alaska—separate schools for Natives and whites and, for many years, a denial of citizenship and rights to vote. This raises the question: how representative was the mixing of Native and white mail carriers at this time in history (1900–1940) and in which ways did Natives and non-Natives mix?[1] This work doesn't fully address these questions, but it does suggest that reliable and sustainable transport and commerce depended upon people who knew the rivers and the country, leaving little room for discrimination against Natives, who could often provide the safest and most dependable transport.

In general, perhaps because of the responsibilities of the job, mail carrier families enjoyed a special position in their communities. It is hard to

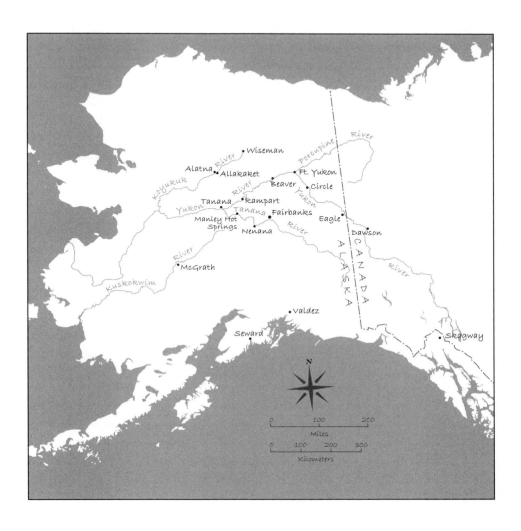

get a read on social mixing because the women and children are not often mentioned in the historical record (Haigh 1996). Fortunately, the accounts of daughters of mail carriers and, in one case, the wife of a mail carrier have made up a substantial portion of the stories shared with me. While my research doesn't answer the question of how the mail carrier families were treated, the accounts have given me an appreciation for the role the families played in supporting the mail carriers.

Over the years, I often heard about the mail carriers and their travels as part of larger narratives of local history, place names, life histories, and subsistence activities, but I had never focused full attention on this part of the heritage. My first recollection of hearing about the dog team mail carriers was thirty years ago when I was living in Beaver, Alaska, with Turak Newman, an old Eskimo man who used to freight up to the Chandalar gold mining district with dogs. Turak told me stories about the freight teams that he mushed out the government trail, "five miles an hour, eight hours a day." His stories introduced me to Kivik Riley, who ran the mail north on that trail, continuing after the freighting traffic had cut back, a time when there were few travelers on his run and he had to break trail by himself.[2]

I never met Kivik Riley, but Turak Newman made his story come alive. When I got to the National Archives to research this book and saw his mail contracts, his was a familiar name amid the vastness of the records that make up our official national heritage. Fortunately, I also found Jesse Evans, the Biedermans, Mike Cooney, and Charlie Shade in the official records. These were carriers I was coming to know from discussions and recordings with their descendents. Finding traces of their work was like seeing a familiar face far from home—just the kind of connection I was hoping to make. In some cases there was even correspondence. With shock and delight, I grew to realize that the mail carriers were part of a paper trail extending systematically all the way back to Washington, D.C.—a world quite apart in terms of the day-to-day conditions the mail carriers faced on the trail, but one that set the conditions for their employment.

The records at the National Archives posed a dilemma. Amid the volumes of records, I had to find a practical way to review the files, and this played into my decision to limit my review to the interior routes and try to record the contracts for each route up to the time aviation took over. This was manageable and gave me a fairly good idea of the evolution of routes but, in many cases, not a full record of each mail carrier who actually ran the trail. This is because the contracts were often written to the Northern

Commercial Company and they, in turn, would subcontract to the individual carriers (Brown 1929). In order to find the individual carriers, I had to draw on personal recollections of who did the work. My research on individual carriers is ongoing. There were the regular carriers who did the job for many years, and there were also a number of men who helped out for a run here and there.

Another reason to focus on the Interior was that I had traveled a few of these trails myself. The contrast between my experience—traveling in springtime, with a small team on a packed snow machine trail, through country largely devoid of settlement—is markedly different from the mail carriers' experiences. They traveled in all kinds of winter conditions, with large teams and heavy loads, and through country dotted with fellow travelers, cabins, and roadhouses. The contrast between then and now played on me and nudged me to dig into the mail carrier story in the Interior and share it with others.[3] More a listener and imaginer than a traveler, I turned to the recollection of old-timers, historical maps, and archival records.

Finally, as I got into the record, I came to appreciate that changes in technology, like the introduction of trucks and airplanes, took time to materialize from the early stages of possible to proven feasible and dependable. The Interior was a good place to see how this transition took place. For instance, on the Chatanika to Circle mail run, toward the end of the era, the carriers used a combination of dogs and trucks, highway and trail, depending on the conditions. While the new technology was adapting to the country, the dogs and horses kept the territory connected and supplied. The adaptability of horses and particularly of dogs to the challenges of supplying the country has not received due attention, and the horses and dogs of the Interior struck me as a good starting point. Historic photos of frail planes on makeshift runways and vintage trucks stuck in the mud graphically illustrate the challenges new technology faced. This research refutes the easy assumption that such transitions were almost immediate.

The story of dog team mail carriers is fragmented at best, teased out of sixty- and seventy-year-old memories, recollections of the mushers' arrivals and departures and the work it took to keep them on the trail. But the story itself is significant. The dog team mail carrier era was a time of greater connection with the land. Those who carried mail along the vital trail systems, and the sparse, tough communities along these trails, had an intimate knowledge of and appreciation for the land that is all but lost today. I have told their story as much as possible in the words of the people who

Trucks stuck in mud. (John Zug Album, UAF- 2010-50-235, Archives, Alaska and Polar Regions Collections, Rasmuson Library, University of Alaska Fairbanks.)

Airplane on dirt strip. (Wien Family Papers, UAF-1980-68-98, Archives, Alaska and Polar Regions Collections, Rasmuson Library, University of Alaska Fairbanks.)

remember those times and what it was like, because they are our personal link back to that time. The story was nearly left untold, but it is too important to let fade from history.

one

Origin of the Mail Trails

To understand the dog team mail carrier era, I had to turn back well before the era's time period to the 1867 Treaty of Cession with Russia, which granted administrative authority for the Territory of Alaska to the United States. From that date until the gold rush in the 1880s and 1890s, the U.S. government showed very little interest in Alaska as a whole and in interior Alaska in particular. The American governmental presence was limited to Southeast Alaska—especially Sitka, the territory's seat of government and site of the first U.S. post office. The post office was established a few months before the transfer of Alaska to the United States. It would be another twenty-nine years before a post office was opened at Circle in interior Alaska on the Yukon (Couch 1957:34, 69).[1]

A few independent fur traders with trading posts on the Yukon, Alaska's largest and main river, mark this period of interior Alaska history. Leroy McQuesten, Arthur Harper, and Al Mayo were the most prominent of the traders who operated during this time. They came into the Interior in 1873 via the old Hudson's Bay route leading down the Mackenzie River and up the Peel River, and then they portaged to the Porcupine River and descended to Fort Yukon at the confluence of the Porcupine and the Yukon (Brooks 1953:313–314). Another active trader was François Mercier, a French Canadian who came to Alaska in 1868 and operated a trading post at the confluence of the Tanana and the Yukon rivers (Mercier 1986:XIII). These men continued the tradition of their predecessors, the Russian American Company and the Hudson's Bay Company, and catered to the Athabaskan Indians who lived on the Yukon and its tributaries.

Harper, Mayo, and McQuesten married into the Native community and raised families with descendents still in Alaska today. Unlike their predecessors, they ranged throughout the Middle and Upper Yukon River, shifting their posts often to accommodate economic opportunities. Mail service for these traders and for the Native population was not seen as a necessity. Scheduled government mail service would not become a reality until the end of the nineteenth century, when these traders were joined by throngs of gold seekers. McQuesten is noteworthy for grubstaking some of the early prospectors whose spadework lead to gold strikes and attracted the mass of prospectors who expected the government to provide mail service. When the government set up the post, McQuesten served as the first postmaster at Circle in 1896 (Couch 1957:34).

Gold strikes in the Circle area on Birch Creek in 1893, at Rampart on Minook Creek in 1893, on the Forty Mile in 1886, and the famous Klondike strike of 1896 swelled the population of the Interior with prospectors from all over the world (Brooks 1953:328, 332, 335; Orth 1971:219, 646, 791). As the traders redirected some of their business to the newcomers, the Natives, who had developed expectations of getting trade goods, found fewer goods and higher prices. This was particularly true in areas where there was a concentration of prospectors and mining activity, like the Middle and Upper Yukon. A striking feature of this period was the large number of miners concentrated in gold-rich locations. These became supply stations connected by trail and destinations for the mail carriers. These centers were also points of interest to the Natives, even though Native people had not necessarily gathered at these places for subsistence or trade before.[2] Some Natives hunted meat to trade at the mining camps; some made fur clothing for the prospectors. Tishu Ulen, who grew up in the Upper Koyukuk region, remembers her dad hunting moose and caribou to trade with the miners (Ulen 1991). Many of the prospectors were quite unprepared to hunt and fish and live on the land. Many of the gold seekers had unrealistic expectations of services that would be available and inflated notions about the ease of striking it rich. Their needs and expectations drove the U.S. government to respond with exploration parties to find routes into the Interior. This led to military posts, a telegraph line, and, most important to this story, the mail service.

Army Captain Patrick Henry Ray is a critical player in the history of interior Alaska (Sherwood 1965:156). In the late summer of 1897, he observed firsthand the problems caused by hundreds of prospectors unprepared to deal with the lack of supplies and harsh conditions. The Yukon River was particularly shallow that summer, and his steamboat was delayed. They were forced to unload supplies and wait for the water to come up. It wasn't until late September that there was sufficient water for him to proceed to Circle. Freezeup was close approaching, and the situation in Circle was desperate. There weren't enough supplies to meet the needs, and the situation was also serious farther upriver at Dawson. Ray had to address the entire crisis. There was no good solution, but he was able to maintain a semblance of law and order and meet some of the prospectors' needs.[3] Based on his experiences, he recommended establishment of army bases on the Yukon to keep law and order and facilitate communication. He also called for explorations to find an all-American overland route to the Interior from tidewater.[4] With unusual speed, the U.S. government responded with exploration parties into the Interior of Alaska and construction of army forts at Tanana (Fort Gibbon) and Eagle (Fort Egbert).[5]

The post at Tanana is one of the places where mail delivery begins to be recorded, though sporadically at best. The post was built in 1899 under the direction of Major General Charles Stewart Farnsworth. Farnsworth's family accompanied him to Tanana and his son, Robert, wrote about their first winter mail: "Christmas would soon be upon us and on December 17 we got our first mail in months. It came downriver by dog sled, first class only" (Farnsworth Family Papers 1887–1911).

William Ballou, a prospector a short distance upriver at Rampart, wrote to his family in 1898:

> The mail service is very poor up in this country and I see but little prospects of its being better. . . . Someone has a contract to get the mail in here once a month all winter but [I] don't believe he can do it. I haven't got a line since leaving St. Michael and I know there is a lot of mail somewhere for me. ("Early Alaska Postal Service Was Rough Business," *Fairbanks Daily News-Miner*, December 11, 2005)

Farnsworth and Ballou had expectations honed in gentler climes, with little sense of the difficulties of building and maintaining a mail system in Alaska.

The earliest mail carriers were entrepreneurs who operated before a well-developed trail system and without government backing. The earliest report of winter mail I have found in the Interior is from 1896, describing how three Native men—Jimmy Jackson, his nephew, and a third man—carried the mail from Juneau to Forty Mile in December. They were accompanied partway by two white men who were eventually unable to keep up on the trail. They all suffered a great deal, and Jackson appears to be the only one who was in good enough shape to be ready to head back down the trail in a week. One report states:

Mail delivery by dog team. (Farnsworth Family Papers, UAF-1972-175, Archives, Alaska and Polar Regions Collections, Rasmuson Library, University of Alaska Fairbanks.)

Miners were so elated at the intrepidity and courage shown in the Indians making the trip at that season of the year, that a hat was passed around in the store, and nuggets to the amount of $150 were quickly dropped into it. (Episcopal Church 1896:265–268; see also Cody 1908)

Another independent carrier, Mike Mahoney, is reported to have taken the mail out from Dawson on an arduous but profitable run by dog team to Dyea in 1897. He hauled two hundred and fifty pounds of mail estimated at about two thousand letters, and he charged a dollar a letter. He repeated the trip the next year, charging the same price and advertising his service in four Dawson saloons (Woodall 1976:51, 73); Cavagnol 1957:587–610).

Starting about this time we get government reports on the mail. According to the Post Office report for the year ending June 30, 1898, mail service to interior Alaska traveled from tidewater at Dyea through to Dawson, down the Yukon River to Circle, and on to Tanana (Weare). A second contract was let from St. Michael on the Bering Sea coast up the Yukon to Tanana (U.S. Post Office 1898:294–295). One of the earliest government carriers on this route was Charles McGonagall, who is reported to have carried the mail on the section from Forty Mile to Fort Yukon in 1897 (Walker 2005:44). At about the same time, Ben Downing acquired a Star Route contract (U.S. Government–issued contract) to carry the mail from Dawson downriver.[6]

Territorial judge James Wickersham traveled on part of the Downing trail and wrote:

On our trip in the winter of 1901 from Eagle to Rampart we followed the only established roadway in interior Alaska at that time, the Yukon River trail. . . . In the winter one followed the main channel iceway generally, though the trail sometimes cut off behind an island or across a wooded portage, thus reducing the distance and sheltering the traveler from the wind. The trail was marked every winter with stakes or branches of trees where it crossed the river, and was thus kept flagged by the mail carriers, who made regular weekly trips in relays both ways from Dawson, via Eagle, Circle, and Fort Yukon, to Fort Gibbon at the mouth of the Tanana River and thence to Nome, a distance from Dawson of sixteen hundred miles. . . . Ben Downing, a tall Missourian, was then the contractor for carrying the mail along the Yukon from Dawson to Fort Gibbon. His division was cut into three sub-divisions, and his teams were no farther than from one of these divisional points to another, when they returned to the starting point. We had met him and two of his teams, when we stayed at the Star Roadhouse at the mouth of the Seventy Mile Creek. Downing was an old plainsman adept at driving both horses and dogs. (Wickersham 2009:71, 73)

As reported in the *Dawson Yukon Sun* on November 14, 1903, Downing was off to mark the trail:

As I will be the one who will use the trail most during the coming winter, it will pay me to lay it out.

Some of my men or myself will be on the road all the time, and every little bend will count up to many miles

Downing's Yukon mail, Eagle, Alaska, about 1900. (Alaska State Library, C. L. Andrews Photographic Collection, Clarence Leroy Andrews, ASL-P-45-1031.)

before the spring comes. It is for this reason that I want to
lay out the trail myself. (*Dawson Yukon Sun* 1903)

Unfortunately, after four years and lots of personal hardship on the
trail, Downing was outbid for the contract by the Northern Commercial
Company (Andrews 1946:15). His story is well preserved and often retold
when people write about dog team mail delivery. One fall, Downing fell
through thin ice. His dogs pulled him out and he hurried on to a roadhouse
where they were able to remove his frozen clothes. Frostbite had taken
hold of both feet, and they were badly blistered. Despite his condition, he
insisted on taking the mail on to Dawson. He is reported to have arrived on
time, but "they say in Dawson that, as he hobbled into the post office there,
his footsteps were marked with blood" (Simpson 1996:24, after McLain
1905:89; see also Ferrell 1994:99–100 for a less likely account).

He lost the contract with the U.S. Postal Service, but the Canadians,
more appreciative of his efforts, gave him the contract for delivery of mail
from Dawson to Eagle (McLain 1905:90). More important to this story,
Downing's mail route was a major undertaking, unequaled in length by
those that followed. Downing's efforts demonstrated an unprecedented
level of commitment and regularity. He built shelter cabins along the way
for the carriers and equipped them with stoves and provisions (Andrews
1946:15 and 1997:93–97; Scott 1997:93–97; Simpson 1996:24; Wickersham
2009:73–75). He is reported to have employed over forty men in carrying
the mail (Ferrell 1994:100). These carriers may have been the ones who
brought mail to Farnsworth and Ballou.

With a swelling population of prospectors and merchants demanding
mail service, the government had little recourse. They had to continue to
build a delivery system to meet the demand.

two

Evolution of the Mail Trail System

Between 1880 and 1900,[1] the mail that Downing and the few other drivers carried came up from the coast, most often from Dyea over the Chilkoot Pass to the Interior. The White Pass Railroad, built in 1900, made this arduous trip easier (Campbell 1902:6). This was the first railroad mail transport authorized in Alaska, a steep but mere twenty miles from Skagway to White Pass (U.S. Post Office 1902). The trains did the climb from sea level to Whitehorse, where transport was overland to Dawson (Woodall 1976:119). The trail between Whitehorse and Dawson continued to improve, and by 1902 (perhaps even a year earlier) the first overland stage left Whitehorse for Dawson (Baird 1953):[2]

> A minimum of approximately 200 horses was required to operate the winter mail stages . . . supplies of hay, oats, and extra horses for relays were maintained at all posts. (MacBride 1953:43–45)

The route through the Yukon remained the main artery of traffic into the Interior until the early years of the twentieth century. A few years ago, I found two U.S. Postal Service maps in the Archives at the University of Alaska Fairbanks that helped me to piece together the rest of the history. One was dated 1914 and the other 1924. Later, I found a fuller set of postal maps, but these two maps are particularly important: the 1914 map marks the trail system after completion of the all-American route from Valdez into the Interior, and the 1924 map shows the trail system after the completion of the Alaska Railroad. Both the completion of the all-American route and the Alaska Railroad are turning points in the history of mail delivery in Alaska.

The 1914 and 1924 maps took me back to Captain Ray. In response to his recommendations, exploration parties left from Prince William Sound and Cook Inlet. The most significant investigations led to the Valdez trail, precursor of the Richardson Highway, and the military exploration from Cook Inlet that went north to Broad Pass near Cantwell, blazing much the same route that was later followed by the Alaska Railroad. These two expeditions would change the course of mail delivery in interior Alaska.

The history of the Valdez trail is tied to the extraordinary efforts of Lt. P. G. Lowe, a member of Captain W. R. Abercrombie's command. In 1898, Lowe traveled over the Valdez Glacier, up the Copper River Valley to Copper Center, and continued north to the Tanana River and on to the Fortymile River. He traveled down the Fortymile to its confluence with the Yukon, completing the first and most ambitious response to Ray's call for charting an overland route to the Yukon River (Sherwood 1965:158; Lowe 1900:591–593). On this trek, Lowe found prospectors in considerable number all the way to Copper Center—what he described as a kind of "starting point, the objective appearing to be the head waters of the Copper and the Tanana" (Lowe 1900:591).[3]

In a matter of a few years and under the direction of Major Miles Richardson, a road was constructed from Valdez to Copper Center. In a short time, the road was extended west to Fairbanks, where gold was discovered in 1902 (Orth 1971:324).[4]

While exploration and road building opened up Alaska from tidewater north, the U.S. Signal Service, starting in 1900 and completing its work by 1903, constructed the Washington and Alaska Military Cable and Telegraph System (WAMCATS). Besides enabling communication from Nome to the continental U.S., the advent of the line helped establish and maintain a viable trail system through the heart of interior Alaska to be used by the mail carriers.

The plan for the line was to connect the military bases. There was Fort Davis near Nome, Fort Saint Michael, Fort Gibbon at Tanana, Fort Rampart, Fort Egbert at Eagle, Fort Liscum at Valdez, and Fort Seward at Haines (Quirk

1974:1). The bases were established to maintain law and order during the heyday of the gold rushes, and the telegraph line was put in place to facilitate military communication. While this was the initial purpose, the line also served the communication and transportation needs of the general population. The line stretched from Nome to Eagle and Valdez. The speed in which it was completed is astounding when considering the photographs that show the amount of trees and brush to be cut and cleared with hand tools, the cabins that were built along the way, and the miles of telegraph wire that were strung. When William (Billy) Mitchell made the final connection of the line near Salcha in June of 1903, he proclaimed that Alaska was now open to civilization (Quirk 1974:6).

Mitchell may have been thinking primarily about telegraphic communication, but the completed project featured a system of maintained trails perfect for mail delivery. Stations were set up every forty miles along the entire line, manned by personnel with dog teams so they could travel the line to make repairs. There were also relief cabins between the stations for use when working on the line (Quirk 1974:7). Today, sections of the telegraph line, the wire, and the glass insulators are still visible from the trail. The Tolovana Roadhouse, built to service the WAMCATS crews on the stretch between Old Minto and Manley Hot Springs, is a testimony to this earlier era and the mail carriers and other travelers who stayed there over the years.[5] An early image from Tolovana shows a cluster of buildings.

Eight miles of wire was strung in this manner, five months before the line was built. (Edward R. McFarland Collection, UAF-1974-130-104, Archives, Alaska and Polar Regions Collections, Rasmuson Library, University of Alaska Fairbanks.)

In the long term, the telegraph line's largest impact was west of Fairbanks. It provided a trail system from Fairbanks to present-day Nenana, then along the Tanana River to Old Minto, Tolovana, Baker, and Manley Hot Springs. Branch lines extended from Manley to Rampart and Tanana and then downriver.[6]

Long after the telegraph line was abandoned, Tanana elder Lester Erhart recalls stopping at Fish Lake between Tanana and Manley to make calls (pers. comm., May 23, 2006). Similarly, Minto elder Richard Frank recalls that people in Old Minto used the telegraph line to call up and down the trail:

> We had a telephone at our house at Minto. We had the
> only telephone in Minto. Five rings was our signal, five
> short rings. . . . And the trader down at two miles below

Photograph of Tolovana taken from atop a cache before the building of the new line. (Edward R. McFarland Collection, UAF-1974-130-86, Archives, Alaska and Polar Regions Collections, Rasmuson Library, University of Alaska Fairbanks.)

Minto, was one long ring, one short, one long, one short. And the trader at Tolovana was three short rings. I remember all these things because anytime someone called, it would go through the whole system. Someone would eavesdrop and all that. And I remember, my mother used to answer the phone and she'd speak English and Indian both to whoever it was that spoke and I thought that was pretty neat. (Frank 1991)

For the early years of the twentieth century, the military road building out of Valdez and the WAMCATS construction from the north and west revolutionized the routes of mail delivery. The port of Valdez became the gateway to the Interior with trails running north to Eagle, west to Fairbanks and Nenana, and northwest to the Yukon River at Tanana. From there, the trail headed downriver to the coast and eventually to Nome. James Fish, a mail contractor and promoter writing in 1905, described the historic role Valdez played as the northernmost point of year-round ocean navigation and the gateway for the trail and telegraph system:

Valdez is situated on a landlocked bay and is the most northerly port in Alaska that is open to navigation the year round. The government made no mistake when it recognized Valdez as the "key city" of Alaska. (Fish 1905:620)

The earliest report of mail delivery on the Eagle to Valdez trail credits Harry Karstens, who ran the mail route in 1898 or 1899. Fort Egbert was under construction at Eagle, and Jim Fish had a government contract to carry the mail from Valdez to Eagle. He hired Karstens for the northern section.[7] On March 16, 1901, the *Valdez News* boasted "the fastest time ever made by the United States Mail Service from Circle City to Port Valdez over the 'All American Route'" ("Fastest Mail from Circle: Record Broken over 'All American Route'").

The trail north out of Valdez was originally directed to Eagle, but when Chena and Fairbanks became supply points for shipping to the outlying mining areas, the trail north out of Valdez was extended west to the new center of mining.[8] Completion of the trail from Valdez to the new mining community of Fairbanks helped cement the shift in the flow of mail away from the Yukon route through Canada and down the Yukon River into

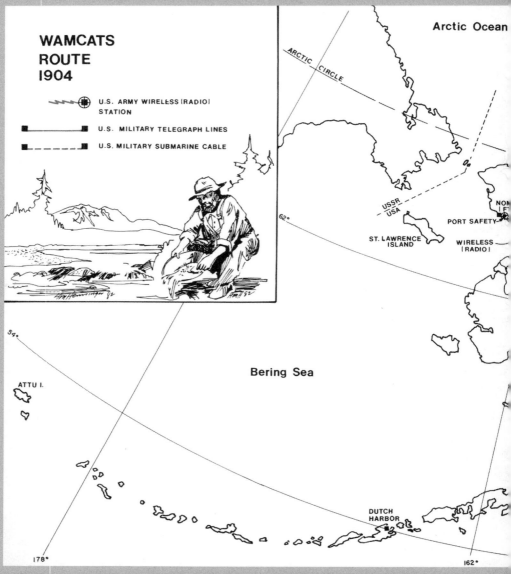

WAMCATS
ROUTE
1904

⚡⊕ U.S. ARMY WIRELESS (RADIO) STATION

■——■ U.S. MILITARY TELEGRAPH LINES

■–·–■ U.S. MILITARY SUBMARINE CABLE

Arctic Ocean

ARCTIC CIRCLE

USSR
USA

ST. LAWRENCE ISLAND

NOM
(FT

PORT SAFETY
WIRELESS (RADIO)

62°

54°

Bering Sea

ATTU I.

DUTCH HARBOR

178°   162°

WAMCATS route, 1904. (Courtesy of the Cook Inlet Historical Society. From *The Opening of Alaska* by Brig. Gen. William L. Mitchell. Edited by Lyman L. Woodman. Anchorage: Cook Inlet Historical Society, 1982.)

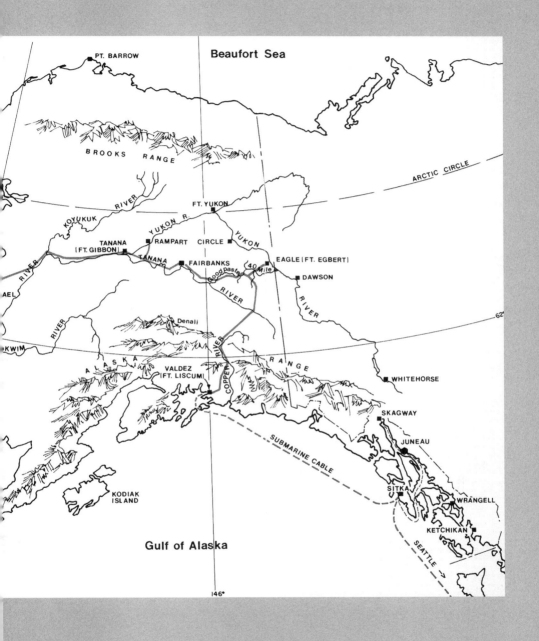

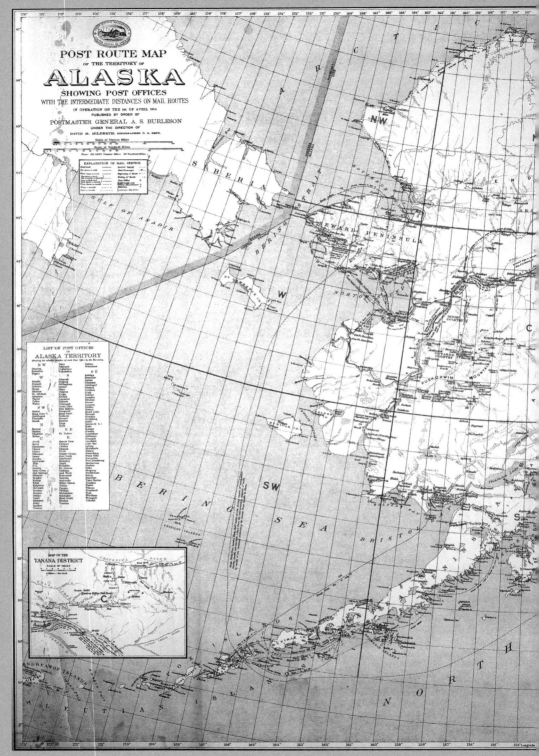

Postal route map of the Territory of Alaska. Showing post offices, with the intermediate distances, on mail routes in operation on the 1st of April 1914. (Rare Maps Collection, UAF MO279, Archives, Alaska and Polar Regions Collections, Rasmuson Library, University of Alaska Fairbanks.)

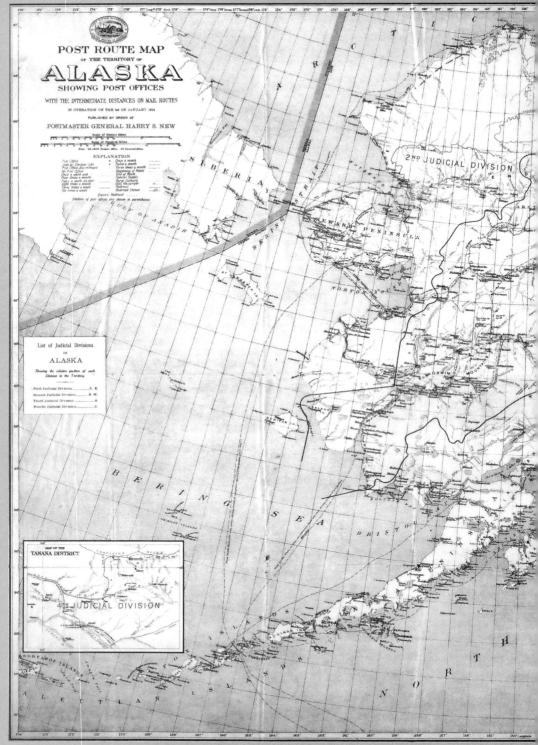

Postal route map of the Territory of Alaska. Showing post offices, with the intermediate distances on mail routes, showing post offices in operation on the 1st of January 1924. (Rare Maps Collection, UAF-05668, Archives, Alaska and Polar Regions Collections, Rasmuson Library, University of Alaska Fairbanks.)

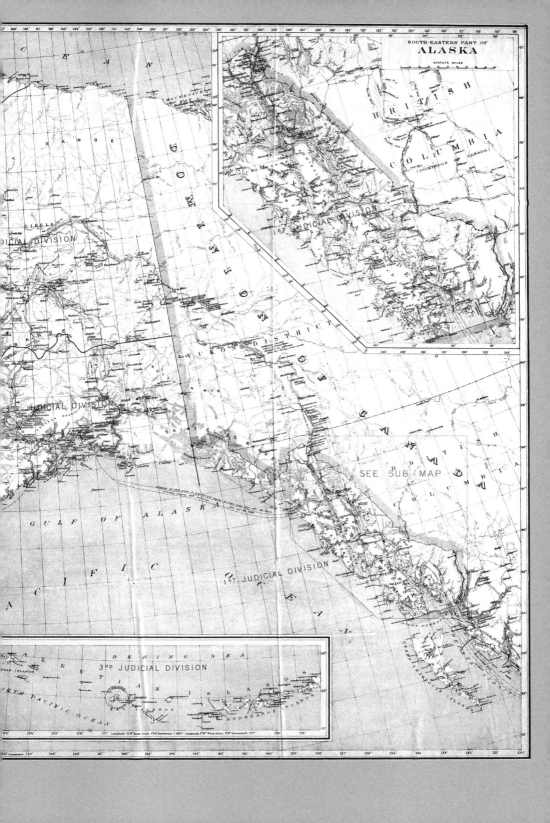

SOUTH-EASTERN PART OF
ALASKA
STATUTE MILES

BRITISH COLUMBIA
(DOMINION)
(CANADA)

DOMINION

YUKON DISTRICT

SAINT ELIAS

GULF OF ALASKA

SEE SUB MAP

BRITISH COLUMBIA

1ST JUDICIAL DIVISION

BERING SEA

3RD JUDICIAL DIVISION

ALEUTIAN ISLANDS

NORTH PACIFIC OCEAN

PACIFIC OCEAN

Alaska, to a shorter and all-American route from the port of Valdez north into the Interior.[9]

At this point, it was correctly predicted that the trail to Fairbanks would soon be upgraded to a road. Fairbanks was poised to become the primary center for mail distribution in the Interior for the next fifteen years.

One of the earliest records of a mail carrier on this route is dated 1903. Harry Karstens and his partner, Charles McGonagall, were hired by James Fish to haul the mail on the northern portion of the Valdez to Fort Gibbon (Tanana) trail (Walker 2005:44). This was probably from the Delta River to Fairbanks and on to Manley Hot Springs and Tanana, a long haul by all standards.[10]

Another prominent pioneer, E. H. Stroecker, also carried the mail on the Valdez to Tanana route. Stroecker and Fred Date were hired by Ike Loomis and the Clough-Kinghorn Company to run the mail from Delta River to Fort Gibbon (Tanana) in the winter of 1905. Loomis (who later became the Loomis of armored-car fame), Fred Date, and Harry Schaupp had run mail from Valdez to Fairbanks during the previous winter (*Fairbanks Weekly Times*, December 5, 1908).

Harry Karstens. (Courtesy of the National Park Service. DENA 1938. Denali National Park and Preserve Museum Collection.)

The 1947 interview with Stroecker is the earliest oral recording of dog team mail carriers I have found (Stroecker 1947). In this interview, Stroecker described returning from a job to slash a road from Fairbanks to Delta. It was the first of October 1905:

> And then when we got back into Fairbanks, why, the Clough-Kinghorn and Loomis had the mail contract, and so he sent me in a small boat with Fred Date to Tanana. We picked up our dogs and sled and fish on the way down. And before we got there we were frozen in and had to sled part of the way to Tanana. And we waited across the Tanana River until the ice stopped running. It stopped at 7 o'clock at night and we crossed the next morning early with big poles and so on. And we had to report there for the mail. . . . It snowed for three days steady; that's what froze the river up at that time. . . . I kept at that all winter long. That was about the coldest winter we ever had. And after that I got into various other things.[11] (Stroecker 1947)

Stroecker went on to become the most prominent banker in Fairbanks history.[12]

At least by 1908, but likely earlier, mail was distributed north from Fairbanks to Circle.[13] This route became particularly important because it linked the two centers of mining. The early prospectors came into the Tanana Valley from the Circle–Birch Creek area on the Yukon River, and when the Fairbanks mining district took off, it was only a matter of time before the two centers (Fairbanks and Circle) were connected. The trail system from Valdez provided an easier and more direct winter route not only to get supplies to the mines in the Fairbanks area, but also to get supplies north to the Circle mining district. The Tanana Valley Railroad was completed north from Fairbanks to Chatanika in 1907–08 to serve mines in the Fairbanks area, but the railroad also carried freight and mail headed farther on for Circle and the Yukon River villages (Deely 1996:58).

Once the mail reached Circle, it was carried up and down the Yukon River, upriver to Eagle and Dawson, and downriver to Fort Yukon. The mail was carried farther to Beaver. By 1931, there was delivery north from Beaver to Chandalar Lake in the Upper Koyukuk country.[14]

Mail probably didn't travel downriver from Beaver to Stevens Village after establishment of the Valdez trail to Fairbanks. More likely, Stevens

Alaska Road Commission map showing trails and roads, 1908–1914. (*Report of the Board of Road Commissioners for Alaska,* 1914, Washington, D.C.: Government Printing Office.)

Map of
ALASKA
showing
ROADS AND TRAILS

0   25   50   100   200
MILES

wagon roads   ━━━━━
sled   roads   ┄┄┄┄
pack   trails   ------
railroads   ┼┼┼┼┼
military telegraph ┉┉┉┉
telegraph station ⌂
wireless station △

Village was served from Rampart, whose residents received mail from Manley Hot Springs. The caption on the photograph below indicates this was probably the case in the 1910–1912 period.

When I compared the 1924 Star Postal Route map to the 1914 map, the most notable new development was the construction of the Alaska Railroad from Seward to Fairbanks.

The railroad was completed from Seward to Nenana by 1923. Even before the line was finished, however, the winter mail had shifted to a combination of sled and train, and Seward had begun to replace Valdez as the major port of entry for the post:

> After the 1920 season the line gapped a mere eighty-three miles between the ends of steel. None of the large steel bridges were built, but breaks in the line were small enough for the post office to shift its winter mail contract

Mail carrier leaving for downriver. Title from original caption: "Photograph of the mail carrier leaving Stevens Village." Narrative in photo album reads: "At the right is the mail carrier leaving the village bound downriver. Before we came mail was delivered thus once every four weeks during the winter. The service was discontinued just the winter previous, so we had no regular winter delivery." (Rivenberg, Lawyer, and Cora Photograph Album, 1910–1914, UAF-1994-70-168, Archives, Alaska and Polar Regions Collections, Rasmuson Library, University of Alaska Fairbanks.)

from the Valdez trail to the railroad. From October 1, 1920, the A.E.C. trainmen took the mail sacks at dockside, then carried them to the horse sled drivers south of Broad Pass, who ran them through to the north edge of Nenana Canyon and steel once more. The mail moved from Seward to Fairbanks on a seven-and-one-half-day schedule. (Wilson 1977:79)

An intriguing couple of photos taken in Broad Pass actually show dog teams hauling between the steel.

With the new railroad, Nenana became a depot for mail bound west and mail bound northwest. Jack Coghill recalls the scene at Nenana: "When the passenger train would come in, they had a green painted boxcar that sat right behind the steam engine and that was full of mail" (Coghill 2006).

Mail team. Broad Pass gap between steel. Winter 1920. (Healas Collection, UAF-96-178-27, Alaska and Polar Regions Collections, Rasmuson Library, University of Alaska Fairbanks.)

Double-enders, or sleds drawn by horses, as well as dog teams carried mail along the Manley Hot Springs trail with connecting lines at Manley to Rampart, Tanana, and downriver (Alaska Road Commission 1929:89). After the railroad was built, a second trail connected Nenana with McGrath via Diamond and went on to Lake Minchumina, Telida, and Medfra. This replaced the Iditarod Trail, which operated as a mail route for only five years (Brown 1980:81–82).

In summer, Nenana also served as the river terminus for steamboats bound for the Yukon and its tributaries. When airplanes took over mail service in the late 1930s and early 1940s, Fairbanks regained its role as the center for mail distribution.

With minor exceptions, the 1924 postal map documents the course of mail delivery in interior Alaska until the advent of airplane mail service. Ironically, the 1924 map was published the same year Ben Eielson made his experimental mail delivery flight from Fairbanks to McGrath and back. Despite the omen of change, and the fact that it was also one year before the lively debate over whether to use dog teams or airplanes to rush the serum to Nome to combat the diphtheria epidemic (Salisbury and Salisbury 2003), it is at this point that the story of the mail carriers emerges most clearly in the oral record and in the recollections of elders.

SIGNIFICANT DATES IN THE EVOLUTION OF WINTER MAIL SERVICE TO INTERIOR ALASKA

1880–1898:	Independent carriers operating on Upper Yukon River and reaching tidewater at Dyea.
1898:	Nome gold rush spurs plans to extend mail delivery down the Yukon River and up the coast to Nome.
1900:	Ben Downing awarded U.S. Postal Service contract to deliver mail from Dawson to Nome.
	White Pass Railroad line completed, providing expedited access to trail from Whitehorse to Dawson.
1903:	The Valdez trail to Eagle and Fairbanks becomes the all-American route into the Interior of Alaska and the most direct route to the Fairbanks mining district.
By 1907:	Mail service becomes available from Fairbanks to Circle with the Fairbanks to Chatanika portion on the Tanana Valley Railroad.
1910:	Completion of the Copper River Railroad from Cordova to Chitina. Sometimes mail routed from Cordova to Chitina to Fairbanks to avoid deep snow in Thompson Pass (Wilson 1977:42; *Fairbanks Daily News-Miner*, September 9, 1916).
1914:	Rainey Pass trail from Cook Inlet to Iditarod authorized as a mail route, but abandoned in 1919 in favor of Nenana to McGrath trail (Brown 1980:81–82).
By 1924:	The Alaska Railroad provides mail service from Seward to Fairbanks.
•	Mail service from Nenana to McGrath facilitated by completion of the railroad.
•	Mail service provided from Dunbar on the railroad to Livengood.
•	Scheduled mail service provided by this date between Fort Yukon and Beaver.
1924–1931:	Mail service provided from Beaver to Chandalar.
Late 1930s to early 1940s:	Scheduled airmail service provided to communities in interior Alaska.
1950:	Last year Percy DeWolfe carried the mail from Eagle to Dawson.

IMPORTANT GOLD STRIKES, POST OFFICES, AND TRAILS

Gold Strikes	Establishment of Post Office	Record of Mail Trail
Circle (trading post established in 1887, gold on Birch Creek in 1893)	1896	Private express carriers operating as early as late 1890s from Skagway to Dawson and down Yukon River
Dawson/Klondike 1896/1897	1896	Private express carriers operating in late 1890s on the Yukon River
Forty Mile strike 1886	1898 (Eagle)	Private express carriers traveling the Yukon River by late 1890s to Dawson, Whitehorse, and down to Dyea and Skagway
Beaver (established in 1911–1912 as river terminus for overland transport north to Caro and Chandalar mining district)	1913	Linked by trail from Fairbanks to Circle to Fort Yukon to Beaver
Rampart (supply post for mining on Minook Creek, 1896)	1898	Linked by Dawson trail down the Yukon until 1903 when WAMCATS line completed
Tanana (trailhead for route north to Koyukuk River and mining at Coldfoot, Wiseman, and Nolan [Fort Adams], 1869)	1898	Linked by Dawson trail down the Yukon until 1903 when WAMCATS line completed
Fairbanks (mining center for Cleary, 1902)	1903	WAMCATS line completed by 1903

three
_____

Life on the Trail

The life of a dog team mail carrier was driven by punctuality in the face of often quite serious challenges. Good dog teams, the right equipment, well-calculated logistics, and an extensive support network made such a life possible. The business of dog team mail delivery extended well beyond the mail carriers to their families, roadhouse keepers, fishermen, and trailbreakers; they all played major roles. The number of people affected by dog team mail delivery grows even larger when considering the mail recipients, those trappers, miners, and small-town residents eagerly awaiting news. Mail carriers rode, if not facilitated, the rising wave of literacy in interior Alaska, and the mail—with its magazines, newspapers, and catalogs—exposed those living in isolated villages and settlements to the "outside" world. The dog team mail delivery trails connected far more than post offices and roadhouses. When the era finally came to a close, the lives and communities connected by those trails changed forever.

HORSES VERSUS DOGS

I originally thought this was entirely a dog-driving story, but that isn't the case. I have found evidence that all but four routes—Tanana to Allakaket, Nenana to Diamond, Circle to Fort Yukon to Beaver, and Beaver to

Chandalar—used horses at one time or another to carry the mail. Both horses and dogs were used on some trails, and horses were occasionally equipped with special snowshoes.

Horses had the advantage of being able to haul more mail and freight than dogs. They could also be used in winter and summer on trails that weren't too boggy, while dogs were only used in winter. However, it appears that dogs were used almost exclusively toward the end of the overland mail period in the winter (circa late 1930s and early 1940s). This may be because the infrastructure of roadhouses was breaking down; it may also reflect a decrease in freight, and it may be an indication that dogs proved better adapted to the winter conditions. This is hard to reconcile with the gradual upgrade of trails to wagon roads that occurred in the early years of this period. Of course, the total number of wagon roads that eventually survived to support auto and truck traffic is low, and when one considers maintenance, it is easier to keep a trail open for dog teams than a road open for horse traffic. Dogs do not demand the shelter or the large quantity of water and hay that horses need. Dried fish for working dogs could be transported on the trail more easily than hay and straw.[1]

THE MAIL CARRIERS' EQUIPMENT

Dog driving at this time was part of the Native tradition, although it was not exclusive to Natives. There is archeological evidence of dog traction from Iñupiaq coastal sites, and by the Russian period, perhaps earlier, there were reports of dog teams in the Interior (*Dogs of the North* 1987; Hall 1978; Michael 1967; Sheppard 2004). The dog sleds were locally made from birch and tied together with babiche.[2] Later, hickory and other hardwoods were imported and used for runners. Plow handles were sometimes used for sled handlebars, and when temperatures weren't too cold, drivers applied iron strips to the runners to make the sleds slide easier.

Charlie Biederman, one of the last dog team mail carriers, described a couple of the sleds that they used to Laurel Tyrrell:

> That sled there, we put hickory runner on it because in the winter time, in cold weather . . . it will stick right to the snow; you can hardly pull with iron runners on, you can hardly move a sled. . . . That other sled we had, that's going

to Washington, D.C. It was all hickory, big, wide. It had iron runners on it. You couldn't move it in cold weather but it was good in the fall and in the spring, especially in the fall on rough ice. Some places we had to go through where there wasn't no trail and that sled would really stand up. It was built strong. Same in the spring going up on the last trip, just before the river break up. So, it would run good with iron shoes when it was wet. (Biederman 1994: sec. 37)

During the period of mail carrying, the harnesses were made with leather or stiff canvas traces attached to big, heavy, stiff leather collars. While some of the harnesses were acquired from traders,[3] some may also have been made locally.[4]

WHAT IT TOOK TO CARRY THE MAIL BY DOG TEAM

Despite the fact that there were some early white mail carriers who appear not to have had families in the country, all the dog team mail carriers I learned about through interviews depended upon a support network to do their jobs, and this help most often came from the family. When Mary Warren's father ran the mail from Chatanika to Circle and was away on the trail for many days, the chores fell to Mary mother:

> It was a hard life, but they didn't realize it was a hard life till they had life easier in later years and they realized how rough life was, but they were all happy there. Her mother had a big family and they all lived there in Circle. So, she was there next to her family and when my dad was gone on one of his mail trips, and I think he was gone probably seven days to Chatanika and back, but she had all the extra dogs to take care of when he was gone, probably when he was there too . . . plenty of work because that was before Pampers and disposable things they have now. (Warren 1994: sec. 2)

Mary Saluna, Kivik Riley's wife, took care of their nine children while Riley was on his mail run from Beaver north to Little Squaw. She made clothing for the family, sewed dog booties, and helped with fishing in the summer:

> My mom and him always cut fish all summer long and
> dry them up so they be dry to feed his dogs with. (Louise
> Hutson, pers. comm., February 2, 2010)

Sally Hudson grew up in a family of mail carriers. Years later at a session
with university students, she recalled the difference between city and village life and the endless chores:

> Of course, there is not too much to do around the home
> here in the city, but in the village there was the water, the
> wood, cook for the dogs, your meals, water for washing,
> and we melted snow, there was so many things, cooking for
> the dogs besides cooking for your own meals, feeding those
> dogs. So, everybody worked in the family. (Hudson 1985)

Effie Kokrine recalled her father talking about Kathryn Mayo down at
Kallands on the Yukon:

> She used to put on snowshoes and go out and break
> out the mail trail so that when the mail team was coming
> down they could hit her trail and come in. . . . They had a
> roadhouse there where the mail carriers would stop over
> night and she would have to have the wood. . . . I mean the
> water for the dogs to be watered and everything, and then
> they host the mail carrier for the night. So, she played a
> very important part in those days . . . she done all the work.
> She was a tough one in those days, to snowshoe out a trail
> in a blizzard. (Kokrine 1987)

The family chores extended to seemingly minor yet important tasks
like making dog booties.[5] Mae Speck, the daughter of Charlie Shade who
had the mail contract from Nenana to Tanana, helped out with dog care.
One of her chores was to sew dog booties out of stiff canvas. In an interview
at her home in Nenana, Mae recalled, "I can still feel the calluses on my
hands [from making booties]" (pers. comm., May 26, 2006). Rose Zaverl,
daughter of Bill Burk who had the McGrath trail run, recalls her mom
cranking out dog booties on her new Damascus treadle sewing machine.
The heavy canvas was hard on the needles, but she recalls it was a lot easier
than sewing by hand (pers. comm., August 9, 2007).

Dog booties for a string of twenty dogs means a lot of sewing, and the booties were only part of the work. Charlie Shade had twenty-five to thirty dogs and would leave five or six dogs at home to rest after each trip. Each day on the trail, the mushers fed dry fish to their dogs. When they were at home, at a roadhouse, or laying over at the end of their run, they could cook the dry fish with tallow, cornmeal, and water. Fish was the main staple and it fueled the team.

Charlie Biederman ran the mail on the Yukon between Circle and Eagle. He also maintained a large fish camp at Biederman's, eighty miles downriver from Eagle. His fish rack could hold 3,600 fish, enough to feed his dogs and the dogs he boarded for other mushers. Fortunately for him, his fish camp also served as a stopover on his mail run (O'Neill 2006:259, 164; National Park Service n.d.). Gordon Bertoson describes Biederman's fish camp:

> Another good place was Biederman's, right across from
> the Kandik, good fishing place there. He had two wheels,

Percy DeWolfe feeding a fish to one of his sled dogs at Forty Mile. (Yukon Archives, Claude and Mary Tidd fonds, #8372.)

two big fish wheels, and great big fish racks . . . and had a
lot of kids, and he cleaned the fish, slit the fish. And they
had a little tram and a winch and they pulled the fish up
the hill and hung them up. And they had a big, I guess . . .
it was a cooker. It was all iron, probably six feet across and
they'd build a fire underneath . . . and throw scraps in there
and feed the dogs . . . and that [cooker] was right in the
[area where they were smoking fish for use in the winter].
(Bertoson 1991: sec. 12)

Frank Warren made a similar point about Biederman's place:

Their main camp was at the mouth of the Kandik
River, which is roughly halfway between Eagle and Circle,
and they put up a tremendous amount of fish every year.
They had fish racks there that were fifty feet long. Two fish
wheels there. That was for their dog team and they sold a
lot too. Well, when you catch fifty salmon in a fish wheel
and you can't keep up with the cleaning . . . that's how
many fish there were. (Warren and O'Leary 2008)

Dog bedding consisted of hay, straw, or wild grass and was put in dog-
houses or spread out on the ground when the dogs were staked out on the
trail. Rose Zaverl described the process:

In the late summer or early fall, he and my uncle and
two brothers would go out to the meadows and cut grass
and then bale it, bring it in and store it up in that loft,
because that was what they used in the dog kennels. (Pers.
comm., July 16, 2010)

The number of dogs that each musher used varied according to the
load, the conditions of the trail, and the health of the dogs. One time
toward the end of his mail-carrying days, Charlie Biederman found he had
too few dogs:

Lot of them we bought, bought from different people.
We had anywhere from fifteen to eighteen dogs. That
winter there I ended up with only fifteen and for a while
it was only fourteen and I had to make two teams out of it.
(Biederman 1994: sec. 37)

The dogs were large by today's standards:

> They'd run from 75 to 100 pounds. That old wheel
> dog, Old Lincoln, even in working shape, he'd be about 105
> pounds, 108 . . ." (Biederman 1994: sec. 34)

The lead dog's job was to keep the team strung out and moving according to the commands of the musher. They also had to be alert to dangers on the trail, like moose or open water. Most pictures of mail teams show two leaders but there were other configurations as well. One dog could lead if necessary, and, in several cases, carriers used loose leaders who ran ahead of the team. Effie Kokrine's husband used loose leaders:

> Loose leader was very important because he was the
> leader and he was understanding of his master, like you
> could wave and whistle and something he would [under-
> stand]. . . . He's a dog that has been over the trail before and
> once a dog has been over the trail, over a trail like Tanana
> . . . over toward Wiseman, once a month. They'd make that
> trip where there was no trail day-to-day in the mountains.
> It's just swept clean, and that dog would follow that same
> trail and then he'd go ahead and the dogs would follow
> him, and if he break off of the trail, why, he can follow
> his foot[ing] and get back on. Then if you want his atten-
> tion, you whistle or go like this and he'll understand you.
> And the dogs, all in the back follow. . . . Crossing a lake,
> they can just go right across and find the exact spot
> where they are supposed to go in [where the trail goes into
> the trees]. (Kokrine 1987)

THE DAILY LIFE OF A MAIL CARRIER

If the dog drivers were at a roadhouse, they could count on water to mix dog food, a cooked meal for themselves, and a warm place to sleep. If they weren't at a roadhouse, they had to melt snow or punch a hole through the ice to get water for cooking. Wood had to be cut and a stove fire might take several hours to bring the cabin up to a comfortable temperature. Roadhouses made travel a lot easier. In many places, the roadhouses could be reached after twenty to thirty miles of travel, a decent day's work unless you encountered bad conditions. Carriers could easily make the distance in a day on a hard-packed trail. A blown-in trail might mean they'd have to snowshoe ahead of the dogs to break out the trail. When snow and wind combined to foul their way, or when they hit overflow or open water, they would be delayed and might have to overnight on the trail. This wasn't easy or pleasant in extreme cold and little daylight in November, December, and January. Fall freezeup and spring breakup of the rivers and lakes posed particularly dangerous challenges.[6] Charlie Biederman described the first trip one fall:

> Sometimes we'd go down the river . . . drift down in the ice. . . . We've got a scow . . . put 'em [dogs] in there and drift down till you think the ice is getting too thick and you think it's going to stop, get out of it then. So they pull the boat out at Charley Creek and then they put another boat in and made it to Circle. . . . Next year the ice was too thick and so we started out, my dad and I with dogs following the shore ice down all the way to Circle. (Biederman 1994: sec. 18.)

In winter, the mail carrier was the primary person on the trail, especially in places where mining had declined and there was little traffic. He had to be self-sufficient, and he had to make his schedule early in the season—during the worst winter weather—and in the late spring when the snow and ice were melting.

Mail carrier contracts called for a regular schedule of on time delivery. A musher waited at the end of each carrier's line, ready to carry the mail farther along to meet his delivery schedule. Adverse weather conditions didn't count as an excuse for not going. With the advent of dog team mail delivery, rural Alaskans were exposed to a new order, an arbitrary schedule developed hundreds of miles away by people quite unfamiliar with conditions and seemingly unmoved by prudent decisions about weather and trail conditions. Mail carriers were expected to go and be on time, no matter what.

Mail carriers were bonded with "sureties" (Brown 1929). The cost of bonding may explain why the Northern Commercial Company had so many of the contracts for carrying mail. They could afford to put up the bond. The company assumed responsibility for the men they subcontracted to do the work,[7] and the carriers were chosen for their ability and sense of responsibility.

The mail system developed quickly and was efficient, but it was costly by the standards of the day. U.S. Postal Inspector William McManus reported in 1912 that there were about seventy mail routes covering approximately thirty thousand miles. By his account, this involved about one million miles of travel (it is unclear if this includes summer steamboat traffic.) The most astounding statistic, however, is that there were no late deliveries to the 144 post offices for the 1909–1910 year. The cost for the transport service, not counting post offices, was $500,000 (Kimball 1912:294). Postal Inspector John P. Clum, writing in 1910, described the costs: "Alaska service involves a maximum of expense and a minimum of revenue to the department. The transportation of Alaska mails is now costing the government between $600,000 and $700,000 annually" (Clum 1910:65).[8]

In 1925, a letter sent from New York to Rampart would travel by railroad or airplane across the country,[9] by steamer from Seattle to Seward, and by train to Nenana on the recently completed railroad. Then the dog

Mail from lower river reaching Eagle, 1906. "Last Mail up Yukon River, April 27." (Alaska State Library, Clarence L. Andrews Photograph Collection, Clarence Leroy Andrews, P45-0601.)

team would take over, carrying the mail west along the trail to Manley Hot Springs and north to the Yukon River at Rampart. Dog team delivery along at least part of this route continued into the 1940s. The last record at the National Archives for this route is for Jesse Evans from Rampart. Evans had a contract to carry mail from Manley Hot Springs to Rampart in 1946, two times a month, November 1 to around April 30, for ninety dollars a round-trip (National Archives RG 29).

LITERACY COMES TO THE NORTH

In his book *The Postal Age*, David Henkin traces the growth of the Postal Service in nineteenth-century America, paying particular attention to the growing mobility of the population, the increased importance of literacy, and the intimacy people found in communicating with distant friends and loved ones through the post. He claims that America of the Civil War period was "literate without precedent" and this was possible because of cheap postage that allowed a new "intimacy over the miles" (Henkin 2006:137, 147). The prospectors who came north at the turn of the century were conditioned to enjoy and expect the mail service.

Fred Lockley, a postal deliveryman in Nome, spoke of the enthusiastic response to mail at the time of the Nome gold rush:

> Welcome is a very mild term for the enthusiastic reception we frequently received. One man on my route was so worried by not hearing from home that he was almost ready to pull up stakes and leave. He had not heard from his wife since his arrival, and he fancied someone with a similar name was receiving his mail. I took his name, and next day handed him five letters from his wife. Welcome! Well, rather. (Carlson and Bill 2007:178–179)

Michael Mason, who traveled in the Upper Yukon in 1922, described the importance of the mail carrier:

> To those who live their lives along the Yukon, the farthest frontier of civilization, the visits of the mail are the only regular events of importance. The mail joins friends far apart, reminds one of another world beyond the spruce forests and the mountains, and sometimes brings in

travelers, who may be strangers or old friends, but always are carriers of news, the most welcome luxury in Alaska. (Mason 1934:217)

Stanley Dayo from Manley Hot Springs recalled the early mail in this way:

> I never spent much time on mail myself; I kept contact with a few people, but I didn't write much. But, it seems there is always somebody howling about the mail not making it in. Old Pete Milovitch, out in Woodchopper, we called him "Pete Million," said some guys would run out to the trail looking up and down for their mail, scream bloody murder if it was late, and half of them, all they got coming is a Sears catalog. (Quoted in Yarber and Curt Madison 1985:61)

Between 1894 and 1907, there were newspapers published at Rampart, Tanana, Circle, and Eagle (McLean 1963:4). The *Klondike News* was early on the scene but published just one edition in 1898 (Doogan 1988:44). Longer lived was the *Dawson News*, which started in 1899 and ran until 1953, and the Fairbanks newspapers—the *Fairbanks News*, *Fairbanks Miner*, and *Fairbanks Gazette*—which began publishing in 1903 (Galbraith and Galbraith 1976:10; Hales 1980:1). The Tanana paper, *Yukon Press*, began publishing in 1898 (McLean 1963:28). The paper had advertisers from Tanana, Nowikaket, Fort Yukon, Arctic City (located where the mail trail from Tanana reached the Koyukuk River), Forty Mile and Fort Selkirk (both in the Yukon Territory), and St. Michael on the Bering Sea coast. I do not have distribution figures, but it had advertisers from throughout the Interior, so distribution must have been significant.

The newspapers provided some coverage of national and international events such as World War I and the Great Depression, and they served as a window to life outside Alaska. Bella Francis, an Athabaskan elder who grew up on the Porcupine River, recalled to her friend Roger Kaye that she enjoyed the *Life* magazines that her father ordered; they represented a world apart from any of her childhood experiences as the daughter of a white trader and an Athabaskan mother (Roger Kaye, pers. comm., January 12, 2008). Minto elder Robert Charlie recalled that Chief Peter John also subscribed to *Life* (pers. comm., November 25, 2008), and Helen Peter from Tanana, whose family was camped near the Manley Hot Springs to Tanana mail trail, recalled that she used to see the *Saturday Evening Post* and *Time*, as well as inch-thick Sears and Montgomery Ward catalogs (pers. comm., December 18, 2008).

Tishu Ulen, an Iñupiaq woman who lived in Wiseman at the farthest extent of the trail from Tanana to the Koyukuk and upriver, recalled to Shirley English:

> We used to send an order in April to Sears Roebuck or Montgomery Ward by dog team to Tanana. Then it went to Nenana and on to Seward by railroad and by boat to Seattle. Our order arrived around the first of July by the first boat. That order had to last for a year. If anyone made a mistake on the order, he would have to trade or sell to someone. In a few cases, the people had to return items, and Sears would honor an order, even a year old. (*Up the Koyukuk* 1983:78)

Most of the Native population in interior Alaska was just becoming literate at this time. In the Interior, the Episcopal Church played a role in promoting literacy. The church established mission schools in the 1890s (Barnhardt 1985), but with subsistence demands, the students could rarely receive more than a few years of schooling. Archdeacon Stuck articulated the problem early in the century:

> Moreover it is folly to fail to recognize that the apprenticeship of an Indian boy to the arts by which he must make a living, the arts of hunting and trapping, is more important than schooling, however important the latter may be, and that any talk—and there has been loud talk—of a compulsory education law which shall compel such boys to be in school at times when they should be off in the wilds with their parents, is worse than mere folly and would, if carried out, be a fatal blunder. If such boys grow up incompetent to make a living out of the surrounding wilderness, whence shall their living come? (Stuck 2005 [1914]:356)

The traditional seasonal round—with the familiar signs of change in season and animal migration; opportunities to travel or intercept game;

or the need to wait on conditions—continued to play a significant role in most people's lives. The new order, with artificial schedules and time-keeping, had its largest impact in the area of schooling. The school year, based on the calendar, didn't accommodate the natural cycle of activity, and many students could only afford to catch a few months of schooling here and there.

The mission schools provided rudimentary formal education to some students, but their services were stretched thin (Patty 1971). Moses Cruikshank, who traveled with the missionaries on their winter circuit, described the routine at night after they made camp, had dinner, and had their dishes washed: "Then I have to study for about half an hour, reading, writing, arithmetic. I got to study that" (Cruikshank 1986:49).

Despite the lack of universal formal schooling at this time, there are some amazing stories of Native people learning to read and write and their tremendous desire to gain these skills. For instance, Catherine Attla from Huslia described drawing words in the snow and copying can labels in an effort to learn to read and write (Attla n.d.). In later years, the schoolteacher gave instruction to Catherine and other adults in her community. But when trapping season came along one year, her husband, Steven, realized that he had to get out on the trapline to support his family. Declaring he had "graduated," he headed out to trap.

Eighty-two-year-old Mathew Malcolm from Eagle Village recalls that he got through the sixth or seventh grade but missed a lot of school because his family needed to make money. This meant cutting wood for the steamboats at a camp on the Yukon River, five or six miles below Miller's place at Sheep Creek. He grew up with a few months of schooling a year but also a lot of time out in the woods working (pers. comm., November 20, 2008). His story is fairly typical.

I have tried to grasp what it must have been like for rural Alaskans to learn about the "outside" world through print and photographs, a shift from learning from experience and oral tradition that is the hallmark of Native knowledge. Walter Ong makes the point that writing, unlike oral discourse, demands a form of objectivity. The words on the page must stand alone, without the opportunity for the reader to ask for clarification—a key attribute of oral discourse (Ong 1982:113–114). If Ong is correct, then rural Natives must have faced challenges in reading about the rest of the world as they transitioned to the written text.[10] It is a stretch to say that the dog team mail carriers brought literacy to the North, but considering that few

Alaska Natives traveled "outside," it is not an exaggeration to say that the mail system exposed people to a wealth of new information in a completely new way.

ECONOMIC IMPACT OF THE MAIL CARRIERS

After the gold rush, the primary source of cash for most people, with the exception of the miners, came from trapping, woodcutting contracts for the steamboats, and work on the boats as deckhands and pilots. By the standards of the day, and considering the limited options, the dog team mail carriers earned good money. Still, the work was very hard, and some of the mail carriers' pay went to the people they depended on for services: the roadhouse keepers, fishermen, and trailbreakers. The carriers took passengers when they had room and sometimes took out fur for trappers and traders. When airplanes definitively replaced dog team mail carriers, the economic impact was felt by the dog team mail carriers' support systems as well. For instance, Sam White, one of the first game wardens in Alaska, reported the sign "Aviator's trade not solicited here" on an old roadhouse wall—the proprietor's only way to protest the impact of aviation on his business (Rearden 2007:162).

Today, parts of the dog team mail trails have been abandoned; others are grown over and rarely used. Settlements consist of towns and villages that are, for the most part, isolated dots on the landscape. Travel between villages in winter is generally by air. A few recreational mushers and trappers keep parts of the old trails alive, and some villages, like Tanana, depend on the old trail to connect with the road system, but on the whole, to use Dan O'Neill's term, the land has "gone lonesome" (O'Neill 2006).

Many youth in rural Alaska today travel farther and more often than their parents and grandparents, with school trips taking them to all corners of the state. But since airplanes serve as their main mode of travel, rural young people aren't traveling through the country like their elders. While their knowledge may be broader, it is less rooted in a livelihood derived from the country. The dog team mail carrier story is a window into the earlier way of life, the country their grandparents knew, and the ways people were connected to each other back then.

four

"Nenana Was the Hub"

A t a community gathering in 1996, civic leader and former Lieutenant Governor Jack Coghill recalled how when he was a boy, "Nenana was the hub." Nenana served as the summer port for riverboats heading up the Tanana and downriver to the Yukon villages. In winter, it was the starting point for the mail trails leading west and north.

I was born and raised in Nenana. I was born in the fall of 1925 and my father was a trader. . . . In those days, Nenana was the hub of transportation for the Interior. All of the mail was delivered to the villages and to the mining communities by sternwheeler and riverboat during the summer months and by dog team in the winter months, and they went to Tanana, Ruby, Louden . . . to the Koyukuk, Koyukuk Station . . . and there were relays that went from Nenana to the west. There were relays that went from Nenana to the south.

John B. Coghill. Alaska State Library Photograph Collection.

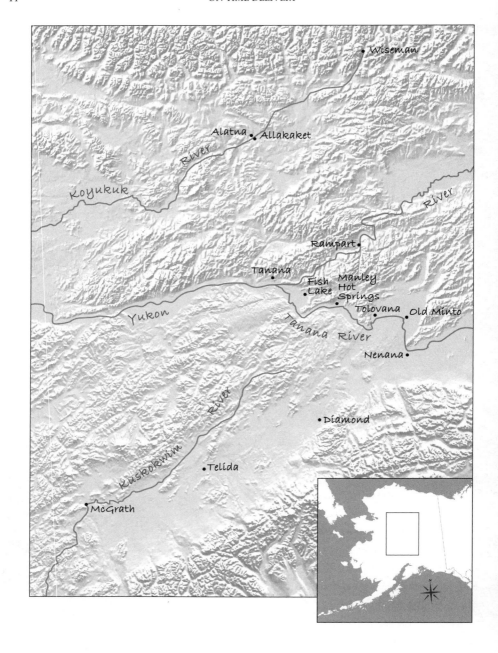

Old Mike Cooney had the dog team route that went from
Nenana to Knights Roadhouse and turned at Diamond,
Diamond City, and another dog team took the mail to
Minchumina and from Minchumina to Nikolai and eventually to McGrath. So, we were kind of a hub of commerce,
transportation, and communication. . . . This was before
airplanes were a part of our society . . . and it took someone several days to come from Tanana and they all came
through our little town, and that is where the railroad was,
you might say, the focal point for all the surface transportation in the wintertime. (Coghill 1995: sec. "Nenana is the
hub of transportation")

Jack's comments reflect a snapshot in time and space—his childhood
and the trails out of Nenana. They gave me the big picture that I needed
to piece the stories together. The next chapter takes up the trails to Circle
and the Yukon; together these two networks of trails are the primary limbs
of the dog team mail system in the Interior after 1924 and serve as settings
for the stories and memories recalled by today's elders.

Years after the Communities of Memory session, Jack fleshed out more
details on the mail carriers and the trails out of Nenana. He saw a lot of
the three principal drivers on this route: Charlie Shade, Mike Cooney, and
Bill Burk.

Charlie Shade's history goes back. His dad was a care-
taker up at the army post in Eagle, and Charlie Shade
and his brother, Ore, were in the service there and got
assigned there and that's how their dad followed the
kids up there. . . . After Ore got out of the service, he
went to Tanana, and he became the storekeeper for the
Alaska Commercial Company that got bought out by
the Northern Commercial Company, and he returned
there as the storekeeper . . . Charlie, who was the team-
ster side of the Shade family, followed his brother Ore to
Tanana . . . probably both of them transferred down there
in the WAMCATS service . . . and he drove horses for
the WAMCATS service and did the supplies and did the
routing of the WAMCAT line. . . . So that's where Charlie
started and that's where he met his wife, Lizzy Shade, and

they started their family in Tanana. Well, then when the mail-carrying became dog team instead of horse team and supply teams, why he moved here to Nenana and started his run from Nenana to Minto, from Minto to Tolovana, from Tolovana to Manley Hot Springs. (Coghill 2006)

NENANA TO MANLEY HOT SPRINGS

Charlie's run to the gold mining center of Manley Hot Springs paralleled the Tanana River, following the telegraph line heading downriver through the sloughs and lakes to Johnny Campbell's roadhouse (a bend below the Athabaskan village of Old Minto).[1] From Campbell's, he went approximately thirty more miles on to Tolovana Roadhouse. The roadhouse was built in 1903 to capitalize on the Army Corps Signal station, put up during the WAMCATS construction.[2] Paul Esau grew up at Tolovana and used to break trail for Charlie Shade. Receiving a call from Minto, he'd leave Tolovana and head upriver toward Old Minto. There, he would be joined by another trailbreaker, Louis Syles, who would be heading down to meet him. Together they covered the distance between Tolovana and Old Minto.[3] From Tolovana, the last stretch of Charlie Shade's run led to Manley Hot Springs. The round-trip took a week, and his travel was timed to meet the connecting carriers coming from Tanana and Rampart. Of course, weather and poor trail conditions could disrupt the schedule and relay of the mail.[4]

We get some idea of what it took to run the mail from correspondence in 1943 between Charlie Shade and the Chief Clerk of the Railway Mail Service. Charlie references a letter he received from the clerk dated October 20, in which the clerk called for a change in the schedule from once a week delivery of mail to once every two weeks:

> As to the hardships that would be imposed upon myself in case your office should decide to curtail the route, there are several. First, I have engage[d] a man to haul the mail for me on the south end of the run, namely, from Hot Springs to Tanana. He is now waiting and depending on this job. Secondly, I have a great deal of dog-feed [s]cattered all along the trail and as you may have hread [heard] the dog fish cost about 25 cents per pound this season. Third,

I have maintained an eleven (11) dog team through the summer at a cost of approximately $7.00 per dog per month and even if the trip were to be made only every other week, the dogs still have to be fed every day, the same as they are now when the trip is made every week. The last reason I will state, although there are others, is that the trip every other week would entail a great [deal] of extra labor in order to keep the trail open as it would not have the regular travel. (Charles Shade to Chief Clerk Earl L. March, District no. 6 Railway Mail Service, Anchorage, Alaska, National Archives Collection)

It is rather astounding that the clerk would call for a change when the season for carrying mail by dog team was about to start and obvious preparations were already in place. Perhaps this is a good indication of how little the government officials understood local conditions and what had to be done. I don't know if Charlie got his way for the winter of 1943, but I suspect he might have. The next piece of correspondence from the clerk, dated August 14, 1944, accepts Charles Shade's bid for service, but just from Nenana to Manley Hot Springs and for a sum prorated at $92.09 round-trip.

This turn of events almost marks the end of dog team mail service between Nenana and Manley Hot Springs. According to Charlie's daughter, Mae, Charlie left the territory to have a thyroid operation, and Mae's first husband, Bill Williams, filled in for him for the winter of 1944 (pers. comm., May 26, 2006).

Jack Coghill recalled that Charlie "was ill, and he turned his run over to Bill Williams. . . . Bill Williams was a steward on the steamer *Yukon*, that's how he came into the country. That's how a lot of those guys came into the country" (Coghill 2006).

A September 10, 1945, letter from the Chief Clerk of the Railway Mail Service describes the following:

As Mr. Charles A. Shade has been released from his contract for service on route 78114 Nenana to Hot Springs, it has become necessary to provide for the following temporary service by aircraft from Fairbanks to Hot Springs. (Chief Clerk to Smith Purdum, Second Assistant Postmaster General, Railway Mail Service, 10 September 1945, National Archives Collection)

Charlie returned to Nenana, but he never returned to mail runs. As for the new air service, Minto elder Richard Frank recalls that you could always count on the dog team mail carriers every week at Old Minto, but it was real spotty after the airplanes came in (Frank 1991).

The Trail Today

Much of Charlie Shade's old mail trail is still used, particularly by recreational mushers out of Nenana. Some people from New Minto maintain cabins at Old Minto, and this also serves as the site of a culture camp and a substance abuse recovery center. The stretch of trail from Old Minto to Tolovana was kept open by the Bowers family, who lived there until flood damage in the spring of 2008. Since then, this section of trail has received less use, but is still passable. The section of trail from Tolovana to Manley Hot Springs is clearly marked with new tripods.

MANLEY HOT SPRINGS TO TANANA

Tanana was a steamboat stop in the summer, and in the winter it served as a transfer station for mail coming from Manley Hot Springs and headed

U.S. Mail Team. (Alaska State Library, Sadlier/Olsen Photograph Collection, Shade, P289-079.)

downriver to the Bering Sea coast as well as mail headed overland to the Upper Koyukuk River gold mining country. Ambrose Kozevnikoff, Edgar Kallands, and Lee Edwin carried the mail on the Manley to Tanana run. Ambrose and Edgar were brothers-in-law.[5] Ambrose had the mail run for nine winters. Ambrose's part Russian and part Yup'ik father, Alex, who grew up on the lower Yukon River, worked for the Northern Commercial Company and also had a mail contract to carry mail by dog team on the coast around St. Michael.[6]

Ambrose's Tanana to Manley run left Tanana from above the old mission. He crossed the Yukon, picked up Hay Slough, and then cut off to Donohue Lake, where Jack Donohue stayed. He kept going on to Long Lake, Fish Lake, and American Creek, where there were some miners, and then on up to the center of mining at Tofty, finally stopping in Manley Hot Springs after sixty-two miles one way.[7] Before he built a cabin to overnight at Long Lake, Ambrose would stay with the miners at American Creek, and that's where they spent the night the time Wilfred "Todd" Kozevnikoff went with his father. Todd's account is through the eyes of a five- or six-year-old boy, but with his memory for detail and skill as a storyteller, Todd recalls:

> I was pretty small then, but I remember part of the trip. We stayed at the roadhouse that still stands there today [at Manley]. . . . I remember sitting at the big long table with people that were there, the mail carriers, and it was sort of boardinghouse style. . . . But they stayed up quite late there. They played poker, all the people, the mail carriers and the other people, the miners who were spending the winter in Manley. And I remember Gus Benson, who was a commissioner and postmaster. And [he] had his coat hanging on the end of a banister on the stairs, and I was sliding down that banister and knocked his coat off, and he told me he was going to get even with me and he had to go home and fix his fire. Of course, I didn't know that, and he went home and got [these] false teeth that stuck out like fangs there, scared the Holy Hell out of me and I be running all around that place. But they let me play the slot machines there. That was another thing that fascinated me. I could never figure out why they never let me keep the money whenever I won, but they give me the money

to put in there. But I think Toots and Dimes Windish were the people who were running the hotel there. . . . They played poker all evening there. And we had rooms upstairs, and dad and I had a room up there. And I think I had my own bed if I remember . . .

And there was an NC Company at Manley Hot Springs at that time, and they had a big barn there, and all the mail carriers kept their dogs in the barn. They didn't leave their dogs outdoors. And . . . the dog barn was as big as a horse barn would have been. It was a regular building with high walls and stalls in there, a bunch of hay stashed in there to bed the dogs down They fed them real good when they get into Manley there, gave them straw, fed them good. And if they stayed overnight two days, well those dogs got two days of rest. And that time, Jesse Evans was bringing the mail over from Rampart. He lived in Rampart and came over from Rampart to Manley. And Charlie Shade came from Nenana to Manley. I always thought that was the longest run. I think Charlie was a little bit older than those guys, Dad and Jessie, but he must have been pretty tough to make that long run. That was the only time I seen Charlie until later, when I went to Nenana to go to school and Charlie was still pretty active.

I remember staying overnight at American Creek. And there was another old-timer stayed on . . . Donohue Lake; his name was Jack Donohue. Donohue Lake still carries that name today. And it's somewhere near Long Lake, in that string of sloughs. . . . But when we stopped at Jack Donohue's place, he had a bunch of toys he had rebuilt. I think he gave me a truck or something, some kind of a toy. . . . I remember we stopped at one of those lakes as we were going home and he [Dad] poured me out some coffee and I drank that and I felt like a big shot then. . . . I must have been five or six, don't remember a lot of it. . . . That was one of the first times I can remember drinking coffee, because, he had his thermos bottle in a big sheep-lined case and that thermos bottle must have been two quarts . . . just hotter than heck.

I remember those miners at American Creek had a little toy penguin that they wound up and it walked across the floor. I thought that was pretty cool. . . . Teddy Gietrick [?] was the postmaster. Ted Gietrick Sr., he was a crusty old guy from what I heard and he give Dad a hard time if the mail sack had any snow on it or anything.

Manley Roadhouse as it looks today. Photograph by Sidney Stephens.

I fell off of the sleigh and he left me behind a little ways and I had to run to catch him up. I didn't remember that part but he said, I said, "I'm going to tell my mother about leaving me behind." Obviously, he didn't leave me too far behind.

I don't remember coming back to Tanana. . . . We had to cross the river above Tanana, and I don't remember crossing that either way, going up or coming back, that's how young I was then, but the roadhouse stuck out; that was a real highlight.[8] (Kozevnikoff 2006)

Ambrose ran the mail until he got sick. Edgar Kallands had the run in 1934–1935, and then Lee Edwin had the run for a year before the airplanes took over, around the time of World War II (Edwin and Luke n.d.).[9]

The Trail Today

The trail from Manley Hot Springs to Tanana is still used. It's particularly popular in the spring, when Tanana holds its dog races, but people are back and forth all winter since Manley Hot Springs is the road connection to Fairbanks. On the Manley side, miners work the tailings out of Tofty in summer and plow about twenty miles of the trail in spring to reach their operations, but no one lives along the trail today.

TANANA NORTH TO THE KOYUKUK RIVER COMMUNITIES

There was mail service once a month north from Tanana to the upper Koyukuk River villages, the Episcopal Mission for Alatna and Allakaket, and the gold mines farther upriver at Coldfoot, Wiseman, and Nolan. Effie Kokrine is key to this section of trail. She learned about the Tanana to Koyukuk trail from her husband, Andrew, who along with his brother, Tony, took over from their dad carrying the mail:

When he was seventeen years old, in those days, he was considered a man and he started running the mail team up there for his dad. Years ago they put . . . three sticks together and make a tripod on the trail. So, when you are crossing the mountains you can have some landmark of some kind. . . . When you're running to Wiseman, it was a very tough trip because the weather is so cold sometimes,

Andrew Kokrine and family. (Robert W. Crooks, Tanana Photographs, UAF-1990-102-10, Archives, Alaska and Polar Regions Collections, Rasmuson Library, University of Alaska Fairbanks.)

and you carried the dog food you are going to use for the
... trip. ... And you're coming back and you depend on
that dog food being there. ... And it took a man and you
had to be strong and tough and you had to have tough dogs
and your equipment, your harness had to be heavy ... so
they don't wear out or fray. ... And then they've got to be
responsible because you're carrying money.

They had relief cabins all along the route. ... It is far
enough when you can make ten miles a day, twelve miles a
day, because you had a heavy load. You had all your equipment, your clothing, your dog food, and everything, and
plus the mail. And coming back if you bought a bunch of
fur, fox skins or whatever, then you have all that to haul
back too, although it is a lighter trip coming back if you
don't have that much dog food to carry.

And then on the side, they used to take like beads ...
sewing bead and sell that along the way too, if you want
to do it. But, that is on your own; that's got nothing to do
with U.S. mail.

Then, if two people go, they can take two sleds, and
the lighter sled can break the trail for the heavy sled. That
was the best way to travel. ... Sometimes it would drift
so bad. ... The weather was just different. Sometimes the
mail carrier had to walk ahead of the dogs with his snowshoes to break the trail out. So, you had to have dogs you
could trust behind you and ahead.[10] (Kokrine 1987)

The Tanana to Allakaket trail, unlike many of the other trails, couldn't
be supplied in summer by river transport, so the mail carriers had to carry
all the food for themselves and their dogs. The Kokrines are the most well-
known mail carriers on this route, but there were others.

The caption written on the photo on the next page, dated 1899, provides a hint of what may be the earliest mail delivery on this route.[11] The
caption is intriguing because it calls these men mail team, but considering
the early date, these men were probably operating without a government
contract (*Up the Koyukuk* 1983:46).

Closer to the memory of today's elders, Joe Beetus recalls that when he
was a little boy, Johnny Adams was the mail carrier who brought Christmas

gifts for the mission and had a white dog called Reindeer (Beetus 1996 and 2004: sec. 3).[12]

Mardy Murie and her husband traveled the Alatna to Tanana trail in November 1924 and found it rough going. Some of this was due to too little snow and a bad spot of overflow (Murie 1997:200–205). Hudson Stuck, the Episcopal archdeacon, and Arthur Harper, his Athabaskan helper, traveled the trail from Alatna to Tanana in January 1910 and experienced wild fluctuations in temperature—a low of seventy degrees below zero with deep snow. It took them fifteen days on a trip that usually takes five. It seems they had to break trail most of the way, even though part of the time they were accompanied by a mail carrier, a man simply called "Bob the mail carrier." After detailing his trip, Stuck went on to describe the hardships of the mail carriers and the folly of a schedule that ignores local conditions:

> So far as there is anything heroic about the Alaskan trail, the mail-carriers are the real heroes. They must start out in all weathers, at all temperatures; they have a certain specified time in which to make their trips and they must keep within that time or there is trouble. The bordering

Jasper Wyman. From glass plate "Koyuk Mail." (Jasper Wyman Collection, Anchorage Museum, B89.24.160.)

country of the Canadian Yukon has a more humane government than ours. There neither mail-carrier nor any one else, save in some life-or-death emergency, with license from the Northwest Mounted Police, may take out horse or dogs to start a journey when the temperature is lower than 45 degrees below zero; but I have seen a reluctant mail-carrier

John Adams and his wife. "He used to carry our mail." (Tishu Ulen Collection, Box 1, folder 44, Archives, Alaska and Polar Regions Collections, Rasmuson Library, University of Alaska Fairbanks.)

chased out at 60 degrees below zero, on pain of losing his
job, on the American side. (Stuck 2005 [1914]:214–215)

The Trail Today

Recreational mushers use the Tanana to Allakaket trail occasionally, and
a few years back there were dog races sponsored between the two villages.
The Bureau of Land Management has also hired villagers to mark the trail
and erect tripods, but there is no settlement over most of the route.

MANLEY HOT SPRINGS TO RAMPART

Located on the south bank of the Yukon River, Rampart supported a population of gold miners and was one of the most ethnically mixed of all the
mining communities.

Emil Bergman was one of the first mail carriers on the Manley to
Rampart run. Originally from Sweden, Emil came to Rampart and married
Annette "Nettie" Mayo. Annette was the daughter of the pioneer trader

Emil Bergman on the Manley Hot Springs to Rampart trail with a nurse in the sled. Photograph courtesy of his son, Grafton Bergman.

Captain Al Mayo and Margaret Neehunilthnoh (Nelson 1995).[13] Emil's career running the mail on the Manley to Rampart trail ended after he was injured in a sawmill accident, and he moved upriver to Fort Yukon where he ran the post office (Grafton Bergman [Emil's son], pers. comm., May 4, 2009). The dog-driving job then went to his brother-in-law, Charles Mayo (Nelson 1995:4).

Rampart elder Bill Roberts listed the mail carriers he remembered on this route: there was Charlie Mayo, Al Woods and his boys, Harold and Walter, and Jesse Evans and his son, Roxy (Nelson 1995).[14]

Al Woods was from Massachusetts. He came up prospecting for gold but turned to carrying the mail on the Manley to Rampart trail, raised a family, and turned the mail run over to his boys, Harold and Walter. Harold and his sister Sally Hudson had strong personal links to this section of trail. As a young girl, Sally made a trip over the trail with Harold, who is one of the few dog team mail carriers on tape. Harold and Sally are key to the history of this trail. Sally begins:

> After my father got started, then he turned the carrying-
> the-mail over to my brothers, who were a little older than I,
> and they would carry the mail back and forth, and dad just

Charles Mayo (Cap Mayo's son) with his children. (Richard Frank Collection, UAF-1873-71-7, Archives, Alaska and Polar Regions Collections, Rasmuson Library, University of Alaska Fairbanks.)

stayed at home with the two younger boys and a girl who was younger than I. (Hudson 1985)

Harold picks up the story:

> It was pretty tough sometimes. . . . You had to haul . . . there were a lot of people along the road and they wanted you to haul a little freight for them and stuff. Sometimes it was pretty tough when it snowed heavy, you know, because everybody wait for the mailman to break trail. Tough going up that divide because it is so steep. . . . We were always loaded, because people always wanted stuff along the road. We used to haul gasoline over and stuff like that, you know. Of course, during the holidays we'd take more than three hundred pounds. There'd be a lot of parcel post [from] people sending to Montgomery Ward, Sears and Roebuck, for all kinds of Christmas stuff. We'd pack it as best we can but that parcel post packs up so high; it's pretty hard. . . . Most of them guys, if they get a little package, you don't charge them because they're always giving you coffee on the trail, a little lunch. . . . The only one you really charge are like the guys that own the trading post in Rampart. (Woods and Frank 1987)

If the trail was good, they could make it to Manley in two days. There was a roadhouse at Eureka and a mail cabin at twenty-one miles out of Rampart. The charge at the roadhouse was three dollars for lodging and breakfast. It was run by "Old Frank Stevens," a miner who claimed he made the best hotcakes in the world. According to Harold, "It wasn't [true], you know!" (Woods and Frank 1987)

On his trips, Harold used seven to nine dogs and in later years increased the number to ten. The hard part of the trail was the steep divide. The wind blows hard on the Rampart side, and there is often ice and water flowing over ice. It was tough going up with a load and treacherous going down, so they rough-locked the runners (put chains around them to slow the sled down). Harold noted that the dogs "mind you pretty good unless they see game," but there could be quite a few caribou on Nugget Creek (Woods and Frank 1987).

Among other things, the mail carriers hauled mail, groceries, fur, and passengers. Sally was thirteen years old in 1929 when she and her friends were headed to Manley for a dance:

> In 1929, my mother was very ill by then. . . . I told her there was about four other young people just in their early teens that were going to go with Harold and Walter on this mail trip. And she asked who was going and [I] told her, and she thought it was a good idea. And we went between Christmas and New Years, because they were going to have a nice dance at Manley Hot Springs. Dance was our big thing. . . . Manley and Eureka, lot of gold had been taken out of there, but there were no children there, so of course when we came they were just really nice. They were just so happy to see young people and we stayed at the lodge, at the roadhouse there, and ate and then went up to the bathhouse, and the commissioner there let us get into this pool for nothing. He usually charged twenty-five cents. I don't think any of us had twenty-five cents. I still have to ask my brother who paid for our rooms. I don't know if they did, and then when we got back from that place there were all these gifts from the prospectors and that was when we all got our first five-dollar bill, never owned one before in my life. And I think I was thirteen then, and the following morning we went over to the NC store and I spent the whole five-dollar bill on beads to sew, and that was really a fun, fun trip, lots of nice memories. (Hudson 1985)

When Harold's dad started carrying mail, he got forty-nine dollars a trip. By way of comparison, I found a letter in the National Archives from Jesse Evans, probably the last dog team mail carrier from Rampart. The letter is addressed to the Second Assistant Postmaster General and dated April 25, 1942. He writes:

> Dear Sir: as I have raised my bid over former contract I am giving you an explanation as for my reason for so doing which is as follows: The increased cost of living is such that it does not leave me what I think a fair compensation. It takes me 4 days to make the round trip and some

times much longer if weather conditions are real bad. My
roadhouse bills are 4.00 per day and dog feed for from 9 to
12 dogs and my increased expense of living at home make
it expensive, so hope you will understand that the raise
I ask for is asked in a spirit [of] fairness rather than just
to get all I can out of it. (Received by Division of Railway
Adjustments, May 16, 1942)

I'm not sure he got his way, but the postal service contracts issued to
Jesse Evans show some increase in pay: fifty dollars a round-trip in 1934,
fifty dollars a round-trip in 1938, sixty dollars a round-trip 1942, and ninety
dollars a round-trip in 1946. The 1946 contract must be one of the last dog
team mail contracts issued for interior Alaska.[15]

The Trail Today

When Sally made the mail run with her brothers, there were people living
all along the way. That's not the case today. The trail is used by Rampart
villagers to reach the road junction at Eureka. The State has talked about
extending a road from Eureka to Rampart, but this seems unlikely with
Rampart's current population size.

"Jessie [Jesse] Evans with mail team between Manley Hot Springs and Rampart." (Richard Frank Collection, UAF-
1973-71-5, Archives, Alaska and Polar Regions Collections, Rasmuson Library, University of Alaska Fairbank.)

NENANA TO MCGRATH

The famous Iditarod Trail over Rainy Pass was the original mail route to McGrath in 1915. The trail was treacherous, more so than it is today, since the mail carriers had to contend with deep snow and drifting, whereas the modern racers have a broken trail (most of the time). The Rainy Pass route was popular in earlier years in response to gold mining in Iditarod, but it was never fully developed because it was such a hard trip. The route was abandoned as a mail route in 1919 in favor of the Nenana to McGrath route (Brown 1980:76, 82). Completion of the railroad from Seward to Fairbanks made Nenana the best spot to head west toward Lake Minchumina and McGrath. The economic impact of the shift in traffic was felt by the road-house keepers. Some went out of business; others moved over to the Nenana trail (Brown 1980:85).

Mike Cooney was probably the last of the mail carriers on the Nenana to McGrath trail. He had the section from Nenana out to Diamond, a small settlement that served the miners on the Kantishna.[16] Jack Coghill recalls:

> And so I can remember when I was a kid looking out the window, and you'd see Mike Cooney going by with two full sleds with maybe fifteen dogs heading for Diamond City. Diamond City was the turning point on the Kantishna where the mail carrier from McGrath would meet, and that is where they transferred their mail. (Coghill 2004)
>
> He would go out, and he'd go to Knights Roadhouse that was on the Toklat, and from there he would go to Bearpaw, and from there he would go up to Diamond City. Diamond City was kind of a stop-off place . . . because of the Kantishna gold rush.
>
> The mail carrier would get his stuff at the post office, and Dad used to send supplies out to Elsie Olson, who was the postmaster at Diamond City, and I recall one time, one of the issues was he wanted half a case of eggs and that would be fifteen dozen, and so Dad carefully got the eggs, and in the morning—early in the morning when they were getting ready to head out the road—why, he wrapped it all in a big blanket, put it in the sled with the mail. And, when Cooney got to his first stop that was the Knights Roadhouse, why, they have to unpack everything, take the

eggs in and put them in the roadhouse and make sure they didn't freeze. And then, when they got to Bearpaw, he did the same thing and then when he finally got to Diamond City, Elsie Olson thanked him very profusely that he got the eggs to him, and he took the first ring out of the case of eggs, that was three dozen. [He] put them in the bowl in the roadhouse and took the rest of them out and put them gently in the snowdrift so they would freeze, so they would stay fresh. (Coghill 2006)

Seeing Olson put the eggs out to freeze, Cooney wondered why he had to go to all the trouble to keep the eggs from freezing on the way over:

"How come you didn't tell me that before?" He says, "Because you had to get that first three dozen to me [unfrozen]."[17] (Coghill 2006)

At one point, and we assume it was in the last of the dog team mail carrying years, Mike had a guy named Archie Holstrum who owned a plane deliver the mail for him:

Cooney got to the point [where] he couldn't do the dog mushing, and fellow by the name of Archie Holstrum took over his run and ran the dogs, and Archie was retired from the military. He was an Alaskan Scout, and he learned to fly a little Cub airplane, and then he flew the mail out and back to Diamond City, and the dog team became history of that particular area. (Coghill 2006)

This would fit with a letter I found addressed to the Alaska Road Commission from Mike Cooney, dated September 1949. He wrote that he had been using airplanes for the last two years to carry mail, but it wasn't working out and he wanted to go back to the dogs.

Gentlemen; here I am again on the Gin. I have been [carrying] the mail to Diamond Alaska by Air the last two years and the service hasn't been satisfactory, so I must go back to the dogs again and the trail is in such bad condition it has made it necessary for me to ask you for help.

It will be necessary to employ at least four men, bridge timber is not so handy as before, I plan on going out myself and I will [personally] handle the work. (Alaska Department of Natural Resources RS 2477 file, "Nenana Route 1947–1950," Drawer 35)

No reason is given for the problems of delivering by air, and we don't know if the request was granted. Whatever the case, Jack Coghill is right: by 1949, the end of dog team mail service on this route had arrived or was clearly in sight.

I got some perspective on Mike Cooney and other mail carriers on this route from the Knights Roadhouse logbook.[18] The roadhouse was located on the Nenana to Diamond trail, forty-one miles from Nenana (Leo Keogh, interview by Diane Gudgel Holmes, Anchorage Consortium Library). The logbook contains entries listing the people who stayed and if the traveler was a mail carrier. After each mail carrier's name, there appears the letters "USM" for United States Mail. The logbook record indicates quite a few mail carriers who have not shown up in the oral record.[19] I was particularly interested in the years 1927–1942, after the Iditarod trail ceased to be important and Nenana assumed its preeminent role as a distribution center to the west. The record for Mike Cooney indicates that he made stops at the roadhouse every year from 1927 to 1940, though he is only listed as a mail carrier for the years 1934–1940. Nevertheless, he was the primary carrier between 1934 and 1940 and he often stayed at the Knights Roadhouse.

Knights Roadhouse Logbook, 1927–1940

	1926	1927	1928	1929	1930	1931	1932	1933	1934	1935	1936	1937	1938	1939	1940
Kalland	4														
Burk	1	18	21	23	13	2									
Milligan	1	20	13		10	13									
Clark		2													
Keogh			3												
Alexander			10	9											
Nelson				1	9	13									
Fry					1										
Hansen					1										
Ritter						1									
Cooney									8	8	3	3	6	5	4
Skookum John															1
Albert															1

Bill Burk, another prominent mail carrier, is also well represented in the record book but primarily for the earlier years (1926–1931). Sam White, the legendary game warden, ran into Bill Burk at 17 Mile Roadhouse, a day's run out of Nenana:

> He was a lean and broad six-footer, and I think he was made of cast iron. He came into the roadhouse after a long day on the trail with an armful of dog moccasins, which he hung near the heating stove, next to everyone's drying socks. His mail was piled on a big tarp-covered, heavily loaded basket sled, with two double-ender trailer sleds hooked behind. Bill rode on the gee pole Ouija board between the dogs and the basket sled.[20] (Rearden 2007:149–150)

The most personal and complete record of Bill Burk comes from his daughter, Rose Zaverl. After Bill Burk's birth in 1886, Bill

> was raised in a farming community called Clinton [Illinois], and he lived there until he was fifteen years old; then he ran off and went to the West Coast. . . . He ended up in San Francisco and joined the Navy at the age of fifteen or sixteen. And he said he got halfway around the world when they found out his real age and threw him aboard a tramp steamer that was bound for the United States. And he said he was never more miserable and abused in all his life. He said he was lousy and starving and they worked the heck out of him. . . . They flung him off the boat, and he said he eventually bummed his way to Seattle . . . and there he enlisted in the Army. And he was nineteen years old when he came to Alaska. He celebrated his twentieth birthday in Alaska.
>
> My dad was a hardworking man, and he came up here originally in the infantry and he served along the Yukon River, and I know the last hitch he served was with the Signal Corps and he was a line man for the Signal Corps. . . . He served three hitches.

When an opportunity developed to carry the mail on the McGrath trail, he moved to Nenana and eventually moved his family there. But they didn't stay long:

Bill Burk in Nenana. (Photograph courtesy of Michael Carey.)

Bill Burk coming into Roosevelt. (Photograph courtesy of Michael Carey.)

When he brought Mom to Nenana, she hated the place. She had never left the Yukon. She just grew up in a small community and she didn't speak good English. . . . She did not like Nenana so nothing would do. . . . He took her out on the mail trail and he put her in a place called Roosevelt.

That lasted until his wife lost two children in childbirth. Bill Burk moved the family back to Nenana, but again, not for long:

We didn't stay in the town very long because Mr. Carlile had a contract with Seattle Fur Exchange to farm mink. Well, he was offered a job with the land office in Fairbanks . . . and my dad subcontracted [from him], and he ranched the mink. And it was a perfect arrangement because there was a lot of land involved . . . and there was plenty of space for him to keep his dogs, the dogs he used in the mail run. . . . There were two men that lived there in the warm barn, and they cooked the dog feed and fed the dogs; not even Mom was allowed into the kennel. . . . There were times when I bet you he had close to one hundred dogs. . . . He had two leaders. I know one of them was named Yankee. I remember him talking about Yankee. . . . He just said he was a "crackerjack"; if it was a crackerjack, you know it was a dandy. He seemed to think the world of that dog. (Rose Zaverl, pers. comm., July 16, 2010, Pioneer Home, Fairbanks)

Another prominent figure on this trail was Carl Sesui, an Athabaskan from the Upper Kuskokwim and a friend of Bill Burk. Several sources have described Carl Sesui's role on the mail run (correspondence from Bobby Esai, August 30, 1906 and September 13, 1906). Carl had a contract to carry mail, and he ran the roadhouse at Telida with his wife, Alexandria.[21]

Telida is located in the Upper Kuskokwim, far from the supply lines and without easy river access. However, Telida Lake is known as a good source of whitefish, and Carl is reported to have caught lots of whitefish to feed dog teams (Peter Snow, pers. comm., August 7, 2006).

Other mail carriers associated with this trail include Miska Deaphon, Fred Milligan, Lars Nelson, and Robert Alexander.[22] There doesn't seem to be much information available on Robert Alexander, but Lars Nelson and

Carl Sesui with wife and dogs, Telida, March 10, 1919. (Steven Foster Collection, UAF-1969-0092-00331, Archives, Alaska and Polar Regions Collections, Rasmuson Library, University of Alaska Fairbanks.)

Miska Deaphon are reported to have run the mail from Lonestar Roadhouse to Big River.

Years ago, Miska Deaphon, an Athabaskan elder from the village of Nikolai on the Upper Kuskokwim River, told the story of hearing a "rattling up in the sky by Fairbanks." He later learned that the "rattling" came from Ben Eielson's 1924 experimental mail delivery flight from Fairbanks to McGrath.[23] It would be many years before the airplane established itself, but the rattling that Miska heard was a forecast of the eventual demise of the dog team mail delivery, the trails, and the roadhouses that serviced the carriers and other overland travelers.[24] I'm not sure if Miska heard the sound of the airplane as an omen of change, but Fred Milligan did.

Jean Potter's *The Flying North* begins with Fred Milligan out on the mail trail between Telida and the East Fork Roadhouse in 1924. Fred knew about Ben Eielson and the plan for an experimental airplane mail run between Fairbanks and McGrath, but it still came as a shock to him when his dogs heard something strange to their ears, and then he heard it too:

> It happened suddenly. All together the dogs turned their heads and looked back. Milligan turned too: perhaps they had had a scent of game. He saw nothing. He shouted impatiently, but now the dogs stopped short and sat stock-still in their tracks, their turned heads all pointing upward. Milligan's eyes followed theirs and he saw it—miles away, hanging in the dimness—a flying machine. (Potter 1947:2)
>
> "I decided then and there," Milligan says, "that Alaska was no country for dogs." (Potter 1947:3)

Milligan knew Eielson would make the run by airplane from Fairbanks to McGrath and back in a day, a trip that would take Milligan and his dogs many days just one way (Potter 1947:1–5).[25] But in 1924, for most of his remote route, Eielson had only the dog team trail as a guide, a faint reassurance he was on course. The end of dog team mail was inevitable but not quite in sight. It would be many years before scheduled airmail delivery was feasible in rural Alaska.

The Trail Today

For a route that played such an important part in Alaska's history, there isn't much settlement or use on the Nenana end of this trail today.

five

Circle and Beyond

Today, most visitors to the historic mining center of Circle travel from Fairbanks along the Steese Highway, over Cleary Summit, past the mining dredge at Chatanika, and up and over Eagle and Twelve Mile summits. Both passes are high above timberline, providing vistas of the route followed by the mail carriers. The road then leads down into Central, finally winding its way to Circle on the Yukon River. While that is the direction of most traffic today, the history of Circle extends back to a time when the Yukon River was the main artery of traffic and transport, back to the beginnings of the gold rush.

Circle was a mining supply stop back when Middle and Upper Yukon gold was the center of attention—before gold was discovered in the Tanana drainage, before Fairbanks, and just before legendary Ben Downing carried mail up and down the river.

Circle's origins go back to the discovery of gold on Birch Creek by Sergi Cherosky and Pitka Pavaloff in 1893. Pavaloff and Cherosky were grub-staked by Jack McQuesten, and their discovery soon prompted a rush to the area (Callahan 1975:128).[1] Unfortunately, Sergi and Pitka were denied the right to hold onto their claims,[2] but their find led others to further discoveries on Mastodon Creek. As a result, Circle became the supply center for the surrounding creeks (Callahan 1975:128; Brooks 1953:332). I was fortunate to work with Frank and Mary Warren and Mary's brother, George O'Leary, on this part of the trail. Mary and George have deep roots in this part of the country: Pitka was the brother of their great-grandparents, and their grandfather, Nels Rasmussen, was a freighter in the new mining district. Their father, Maurice O'Leary, was a mail carrier, first with horses and then with dog teams. In later years, Maurice's mail run partners were Walter Jewell and Walter Roman. All three men were married to Rasmussen sisters. It's hard to imagine a family with more historical background in this region.

In 1895, Circle had a population of five hundred people (Brooks 1953:332). The post office was established in 1896 (Couch 1957:34), probably in the trading post that its first postmaster, Leroy Jack McQuesten, built back in 1887 (Orth 1971:219). Circle was central to mail distribution on the Yukon, both at first, in the few years when the mail flowed primarily up and down the Yukon, and later, when Fairbanks developed into a large-scale mining center and the route between Circle and Fairbanks connected the two centers of commerce. The Fairbanks to Circle run continued to be important until airmail took over. The run supplied mail to the network of routes up and down the Yukon and the Porcupine River and even up into the Upper Koyukuk country from Beaver.

Walter Jewell on mail trail over Eagle Summit. (O'Leary Collection, 2011-25-5, Archives, Alaska and Polar Regions Collections, Rasmuson Library, University of Alaska Fairbanks.)

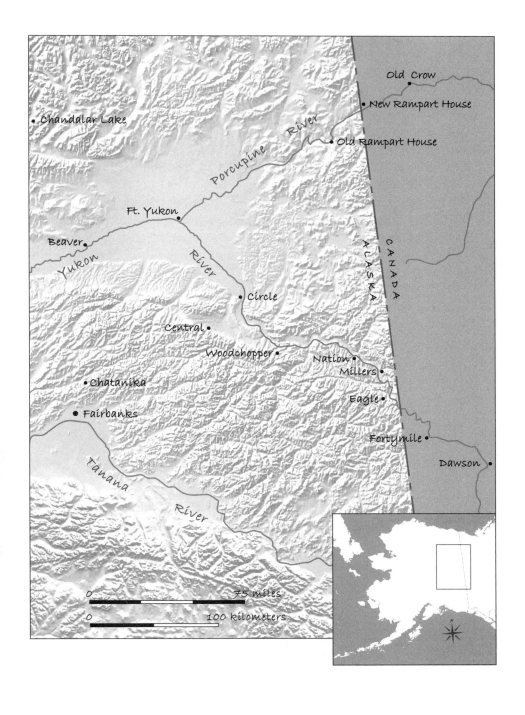

FAIRBANKS TO CIRCLE

The first leg of the mail run from Fairbanks to Circle was on the Tanana Valley Railroad, a pioneer line offering service to Chatanika.[3] Beyond Chatanika, Twelve Mile Summit and Eagle Summit were the big barriers. At 3,624 feet, Eagle Summit was a formidable challenge. Deep, blowing snow, few landmarks, and steep terrain could make this route treacherous. One only has to read reports of modern-day Yukon Quest mushers to get a sense for how difficult the summit can be.

Both Eagle and Twelve Mile were negotiated to the east of the existing road; the trail was perhaps slightly easier than the road but still required rough-locking on the descents as well as stops to rest the teams on the way up the hills. Walter Roman, who regularly made the run, said it all in the label he put on this photograph.

Today, the history of the Circle to Chatanika mail run is most directly associated with Johnny Palm, Maurice O'Leary, Walter Roman, and Walter Jewell. The best-documented early carrier was Johnny Palm.[4]

Johnny was no newcomer to the mail business; the National Archives has a record showing he had the contract in 1918 from Fort Yukon to

Going up Eagle Summit, "the trail that stands on end." (Walter Roman Collection, UAF-2010-0004-00015, Archives, Alaska and Polar Regions Collections, Rasmuson Library, University of Alaska Fairbanks.)

Circle and in 1926 from Eagle to Circle. In 1931, he had the Fort Yukon to Circle and Fort Yukon to Beaver runs. Of course, Palm may have subcontracted out a lot of this work. Johnny Palm used dogs, horses, and finally, according to Sam White, trucks (Rearden 2007:189).

Born in Sweden, Johnny Palm came to Alaska during the 1898 gold rush, hauling mail and assigning Postal Service contracts to mail carriers for the Northern Commercial Company.[5] When he died in 1953, his ashes were spread on Eagle Summit along the highway he traveled so often carrying mail and freight (*Fairbanks Daily News-Miner* 1953a, 1953b).

Robert Redding, who grew up in Chatanika, recalled that his stepdad, Willard Hansen, got a subcontract from Palm for winter mail delivery between Chatanika and Circle in the early 1930s. They were using horses when Hansen got the job:

> Johnny formerly carried this route himself, but had frozen his hands so badly in a blizzard on Twelve Mile Summit that he was forced to give up teamstering. He negotiated with dad and the two continued their association until the spring of 1935.[6] (Redding n.d.:11)

They started off with horses on this trail but switched to dogs when the roadhouses began to close down (Biederman 1994; Warren 1994: sec. 24). According to Charlie Biederman, who had the mail run from Circle to Eagle, the tough winter of 1936 forced carriers to switch from horses to dogs. The Chatanika to Circle carriers had a very difficult time getting the mail through because the horses couldn't get through the heavy snow on the summits. Dogs, on the other hand, could deal with the cold and didn't need a warm barn at night. Walter Roman recalled the switch:

> We had horses for a few years, but then we lost our horses and went to using dogs and Walter Jewell and I and Maurice O'Leary were partners on that for several winters. (Roman 1983: sec. 4)

It is easy to see how dogs would be better adapted to deal with extreme temperatures and deep snow, but it also seems that the amount of traffic and commerce on the route would influence whether it was profitable to have roadhouses and barns to accommodate horses.[7] By the 1930s, reliable trucks were becoming available. In a 1937 newspaper article, Johnny Palm reports:

Trucks now take the mail from Fairbanks to a point twenty miles beyond Chatanika and from that point they are carried by the dog teams . . .

Walter Roman mushes the teams on this end of the trail to a point this side of Eagle Summit. There he meets and transfers the mail to a team in charge of Walter Jewel, and from there on, Jewel drives the dogs to Miller House. Between Miller House and Circle Springs, the mail again is handled by truck. (*Fairbanks Daily News-Miner* 1937)

George O'Leary recalled that his dad, Maurice, got involved in carrying the mail:

He moved to Circle and married my mother [Elsie Rasmussen]. He had a good dog team that time so he was always in demand. . . . I think the NC must have had the primary contract, and guys like Johnny Palm, who was in the freighting business and had trucks at that time in the '30s, probably hauled mail in the '30s and hauled freight for like the Berry Company or other people, but he had the

Walter Roman Collection, UAF-2010-0004-00007, Archives, Alaska and Polar Regions Collections, Rasmuson Library, University of Alaska Fairbanks.

year round subcontract and my dad was driving trucks for
him and then maybe that worked out that he got involved
in the mail carrying in the winter time. (Warren and
O'Leary 2008)

George O'Leary traveled with his dad in 1938 or 1939 on one of the
last dog team runs before the airplanes took over the Fairbanks to Circle
mail route.

> It was kind of a springtime trip, good weather, end of
> March or April, beautiful weather all the way. We went over
> the hill and stayed there at 101 Mile that night and then
> back over to Miller House and then back to Central. . . .
> Probably my dad took the dogs into Circle. When I came
> out to go on that trip, I rode out with Walter Jewell and his
> wife, Ida, and it was another beautiful spring day, took us
> probably, what, thirty-two miles, about probably five or six
> hours and it was easy trip, easy going.

When I asked him about negotiating the summits, he said:

> Well, it is like they do today with the Quest, you're
> climbing out of the other side, north side coming up, you
> have to stop and hold the break and hold the dogs so every-
> thing don't slide back and give them a break, maybe four or
> five times to get over the hill, and then you put the rough
> locks on to go down the other side.

On the dogs:

> I think they had up to eight or nine or ten big dogs, not
> these little poodles they run in the Quest, see, they're forty-
> to forty-five-pound dogs, and they had dogs I think were
> over one hundred pounds and big, lots of fur. You could
> tie them outdoors, fifty- to sixty-below weather, and they'd
> survive, see. And feed them half a salmon every day. When
> they were back in camp, Central and Circle, they always
> cooked for the dogs the cornmeal, rice, fish, whatever they
> had. (Warren and O'Leary 2008)

Maurice used a loose leader named Yukon, the "best dog he ever had . . . he could guide them over the summit in a storm," and when Maurice needed to stop, Yukon would "just lay down and hold the team in place" (Mary Warren, pers. comm., July 15, 2010).

Maurice O'Leary and Walter Jewell had the run from Circle to Fish Creek, where they met Walter Roman, who was coming from Chatanika. Walter Roman carried the mail from 1933 or 1934 until 1940, about when the airplanes got the contract. Roman shared his story with Jane Williams:

> It started in about '33. I took Johnny Palm's interest in it. He and Willard Hansen were running the mail between Chatanika and Circle then. And then we had a short side trip into Circle Hot Springs. And there was mail coming in from Eagle to Circle and from Fairbanks to Circle and then downriver was Curly Wells. He had a mail team, and they'd all be there the same night, you know. (Roman 1983: sec. 4)

Ron Roman recalled a bit more of his dad's history.

> He grew up in Oklahoma and Texas. His mom came across the "Trail of Tears," so he was part Cherokee so

Maurice O'Leary's loose leader, Yukon, leading the team up the trail. (O'Leary Collection, UAF-2011-25-2, Alaska and Polar Regions Collections, Rasmuson Library, University of Alaska Fairbanks.)

basically kind of grew up around the ranching, then started firing on the locomotives and went across the states, and he started working pretty young, his father died, passed on, and they had a pretty big family so he elected to work to help support the family. So, he actually fired on the locomotives all across the United States, learned the steam and coal, and of course when he came up here, Tony Zimmerman put him to work right away because he was a fireman and he knew coal and knew wood and got out, I guess on the Sourdough Creek, in the 1920, '29, '30, the season there. And he said he could not believe the gold they got. He just got gold fever. . . . They were getting nine hundred to one thousand dollar cleanups and, you know, life was good. And, of course, the Depression was on out-side and here there were lots of caribou, tens of thousands of caribou, so you could work for a miner, and then he got his passion for prospecting, and, of course, the mail kind of helped him at that time make it through that so he had money to prospect.

Dad talked about a lot of time one thousand to eleven hundred pounds of mail . . . part of it was the mail and part of it was they made money on the side; you know they'd haul different groceries or different supplies, special things for their customers. So he would meet them at different roadhouses, and they were happy to see him, and they'd tell him different stories so dad loved that. He was in the prospecting stage then, and to be able to talk to some of the miners and hear their history, and, you know, he kind of fell in love with the mining side, but the mail kind of kept him going when he was still prospecting. (Ron Roman, pers. comm.)

The three men coordinated their schedules. Maurice had his place at Circle, Walter Jewell lived at Central, and Walter Roman was coming from Chatanika. Maurice would leave from Circle and overnight with Walter Jewell before they both headed over the hills to Fish Creek to meet Walter Roman. George O'Leary recalled:

The sled bag on the back bears the initials "W.R." for Walter Roman. (Walter Roman Collection, UAF2010-0004-00016, Archives, Alaska and Polar Regions Collections, Rasmuson Library, University of Alaska Fairbanks.)

William O'Leary with truck and dogs. (O'Leary Family Collection, UAF-2011-25-49, Archives, Alaska and Polar Regions Collections, Rasmuson Library, University of Alaska Fairbanks.)

> And if the road was open, like in the fall of the year, they could drive a truck. Sometimes they'd haul the dogs to Circle or Central or vice versa. But when snow got deeper they had to use dogs. . . . I think from Central they could make it all the way to Fish Creek . . . and if the road was open, they could haul the dogs to Miller House and unload there. And, of course, that would be a short trip over the hill. (Warren and O'Leary 2008)

They could find shelter from bad weather in various places on the way out of Central, but George O'Leary thought they probably stayed most often at Fish Creek. That's where they met Walter Roman, who came over the next morning from Twelve Mile Roadhouse at Reed Creek, mile 89 on the road. They exchanged mail bags and headed back on their respective trails.[8]

The Trail Today

Parts of the Circle trail are used by the Yukon Quest Sled Dog Race each spring and the highway is kept open year-round for vehicle traffic. However, no one runs this route as often as these winter dog team mail carriers did, and Circle is no longer the hub of transportation it once was.

CIRCLE TO FORT YUKON

As Grace Marks recalls from her time in Fort Yukon, Curly Wells would come sweeping down the street with the mail from Circle every Friday between 2 and 3 p.m. (Kari Marks, daughter of Grace Marks, pers. comm., August 21, 2008). Curly's son, Jimmy, said that his dad would take three days each way and would run nine or ten dogs. Jimmy recalls the benefit of a dad who ran the mail. When his dad was hauling the mail, Jimmy was "probably the only kid who had apples and oranges at Christmas." That was because his dad brought them from Circle wrapped in a feathered blanket in the mail sled (pers. comm., May 4, 2009). The precious fruit probably traveled by steamship from Seattle to Seward, by train to Fairbanks and on to Chatanika, and then by dog sled to Circle, where Curly picked it up.

Curly Wells also had a loose leader named Rooster.[9] The story is that when Curly got about ten miles out from Fort Yukon on the trip home, Rooster would take off for the post office. Catching sight of Rooster was the first sign Curly would soon be in with the mail.[10]

In the fall, Curly would arrange to supply his mail cabins. He barged in supplies to the Forty-Five Mile cabin and stored food there until after freezeup, when he could freight the food for himself and the dogs up to the other cabins he would use on his way to Circle.

From Jimmy's account, Curly Wells came into the country from Oklahoma where he was working on a ranch. He traveled north with the ranch owner's son and decided to stay in Alaska. He married Elizabeth, an Athabaskan woman from Fort McPherson, and raised a family. He ran the mail in the 1930s. The airplanes took over around the time Curly got sick in the 1940s (Jimmy Wells, pers. comm., September 12, 2006).[11]

It may well be that Curly ran the mail even before the 1930s, since a 1922 account of Harry Anthony carrying the mail credits Curly, who was trapping that winter, with being the regular mail carrier. Michael Mason, a writer, did the mail run with Harry Anthony. Mason wrote that the trip was a tough one because of bad ice conditions, but their overnight with Curly Wells and his family in their camp along the trail seems to have been some reprieve:

> We spent the night there and Elizabeth treated us to cookery which could not be surpassed in a Paris restaurant.

Curly Wells with his mail team leaving Fort Yukon. (Photo courtesy of Grafton Bergman.)

Happy and tight-bellied, we stretched out on the floor in our fur blankets and slept on the welcome thought that tomorrow was only a ten-mile run and that on the night after we should reach Circle.

As it happened, that ten miles took us from long before dawn till nearly midnight, and when we reached our objective, a wood-cutter's cabin on the "Sarah Slough," we had as many falls, through the thin ice and on the rough ice, as either of us wanted. (Mason 1934:226)

In 1940, Harry Anthony was living in Vancouver, British Columbia, and told the local newspaper about his time carrying the mail. He reported losing the job when the authorities found out he wasn't a United States citizen: "'It must have leaked back to postal headquarters,' said Harry reminiscently. 'For they suddenly put the clamps on me and out I went'" (Norman Cribbens 1940).[12]

As for the end of dog team mail on this trail, the National Archives records show that Wien Airlines had the Circle to Fort Yukon and Beaver route in 1938, but the postal map does not show a direct route from Fairbanks to Fort Yukon until 1940. As in other cases, I suspect that there

Harry Anthony's dog team hooked to a sled and ready to go. (Dr. Ernest A. Cook Collection, UAF-2003-109-103, Archives, Alaska and Polar Regions Collection, Rasmuson Library, University of Alaska Fairbanks.)

could have been overlap between airplane and dog team service. There was no overland mail trail from Circle to Fort Yukon or from Circle to Eagle on the 1947 postal map, a sure mark of the end of dog team mail.

The Trail Today

Usually there is very little travel on this section of the Yukon River, although part of a dog race in spring 2011 covered this stretch of river.

FORT YUKON TO BEAVER

Though there are records of a Circle to Fort Yukon to Beaver contract for 1926 and 1934 (possibly with Harry Anthony), no particular drivers are listed in the National Archives. Relatives and elders in Fort Yukon report that two partners, John Stevens and "Big Steve" (Steven John), had this run as well as the mail run from Fort Yukon to New Rampart House.[13] Katherine Peter recalls her stepbrother John carrying the mail:

John Stevens. Katherine Peter and John Stevens were both raised by Chief Esias and Katherine Loola (Peter 2001:39). (Photograph courtesy of John's son, Bill Stevens. Photo also appears in Peter 2001:23.)

My older brother, John Stevens, used to carry mail to Beaver, Alaska, and back to Fort Yukon. During that time his mother made a lot of dog booties for his dogs. She made these booties for the dogs to wear to prevent the animals' feet from being cut by the ice crystals on the river. For John's snack, she also baked a lot of biscuits. Even though John had a wife, she helped in this way. (Peter 2001:45)

The Trail Today

I don't know of any overland winter travel that takes place recently between Fort Yukon and Beaver.

BEAVER TO CHANDALAR LAKE

Beaver was originally settled as the river terminus to supply the mining activity in the Upper Koyukuk and Chandalar Lake areas. Unlike other communities on the Yukon River, the population consisted mostly of Natives: Eskimos from the Arctic Coast and the Kobuk River as well as Athabaskans from the communities up- and downriver and a few White trappers. A government trail was built north from Beaver with small shelter cabins spaced at a day's travel (Schneider 1976; Department of the Interior 1975). Beaver was my introduction to Turak Newman, who freighted with dogs out of Beaver and up the Chandalar mining district. Turak often talked about Kivik Riley and how he had to break trail alone in the last years of the dog team mail, when the traffic on the trail had dwindled with the decline in mining. Kivik Riley, originally from Barrow, is the only driver listed for the route from Beaver to Chandalar Lake.[14] His daughter, Louise Hutson, recalled:

When he moved to Beaver, Frank Yasuda put him to work to carry mail to Little Squaw mining camp . . . fifteen days round-trip, seven days up, seven days back. He rested dogs one day then came back. It's a hundred miles one way, a hundred and ten miles or so. . . . He start early in the fall and stop when there's no more snow for dog team and he did it all winter. . . . Dad died of an enlarged heart. . . . I remember Frank Yasuda used to order him pills. He take little white pills every day to keep going.[15] (Pers. comm., January 2, 2010)

The Trail Today

By the time Kivik Riley quit running mail, the government road was fading into disuse. Some parts of this trail are still used by people in Beaver for trapping, but the upper sections are rarely visited and much of the trail has been overgrown.

FORT YUKON TO NEW RAMPART HOUSE

John Stevens and Big Steve are the men most often associated with this mail run, although there were others.[16] Big Steve and John Stevens had a

Kivik Riley and his wife, Mary Saluna. (Photo courtesy of his daughter, Louise Hutson.)

Big Steve and Anges [Agnes?] Hamilton. (Maggie Cadzow Beach Collection, UAF-1991-138-2, Archives, Alaska and Polar Regions Collections, Rasmuson Library, University of Alaska Fairbanks.)

place partway up the trail called Niche Village, and they would trap some on their mail run (Clarance Alexander, grandson of Big Steve, pers. comm., May 5, 2009).[17] They would take bales of dry fish up the Porcupine River in summer by boat to be used in winter for dog feed. Each bale weighed about fifty pounds and contained fifty-two fish. They would drop bales off at Schuman House, Old Village, Old Rampart House, and New Rampart House (Joe Herbert, pers. comm., September 9, 2009).[18]

Bella Francis, who grew up and spent many years of her life at Old Rampart House on the Porcupine River, recalled that the mail would come in to her father's store. There were lots of magazines for her father, letters from relatives, and some clothes (Francis 1993).

Doris Ward's family lived about fifty miles from the border on the American side, on a big bend of the Porcupine River. The mail carriers made a shortcut straight across to avoid the long way around the bend. When their trail finally hit the river again, the Ward family had a tripod set up for the mail carrier to hang their mail. They could use binoculars from their house to see if their mail had been delivered (Doris Ward, pers. comm., July 11, 2009).

Up at the border at New Rampart House, the Canadians had a wireless communication between New Rampart House and Old Crow. When they heard the mail had arrived in New Rampart House, the Mounties would come down to pick it up (Fred Thomas, pers. comm., May 4, 2009).

The Trail Today

Portions of this trail are still used by people back and forth from Fort Yukon to Chalkyitsik. Some even travel all the way up to Old Crow from Fort Yukon.

CIRCLE TO EAGLE

The mail run upriver from Circle to Eagle and on to Dawson is probably the best known and most publicized of all the dog team mail routes (Nelson 1997; Scott 1997; Skilbred 1998; O'Neill 2006:158; Webb 1983:373–377; Biederman 1994). The first leg, Circle to Eagle, is clearly identified with the Biedermans—Adolf (Ed) and his sons Horace and Charlie—although Johnny Palm may have been the carrier on this run before the Biedermans (Boquist 1991: sec. 9). Ed Biederman was from Bohemia, and after coming to the states, acquiring his citizenship, and a bit of travel, he came to Alaska and began working for the Northern Commercial Company. Ed had the mail run in 1901 from St. Michael upriver as far as Circle, and in 1912 he had the Circle to Eagle contract.[19]

Ed married Bella Roderick from Medicine Lake, the granddaughter of the famous Yukon Flats chief Shahnyaati (Scott 1997:102; Biederman 1994: sec. 27). Ed carried the mail until he froze his feet in 1925 and had to give up the run. The Biederman family, including sons Horace and Charlie, were the principal carriers on this route until 1938 when airplanes took over.[20]

Horace recalled at a gathering of the Tanana-Yukon Historical Society in 1965:

> What little schooling I had was right there at Eagle. When I was fifteen years old, [my] old man took me out of school and put me on the mail run between Eagle and Circle. How this came about, he froze his feet the year before on the fifth of January, right out of Circle there, and he had to have his feet amputated, so the following year he took me out of school to finish out the contract. It was in 1925, '26, the winter of 1925–26. (Biederman 1965)

The contracts ran from the first of November, so the Biedermans had to deal with running ice on the early trips. Charlie recalled how his father always made the first trip of the year when the river was most dangerous:

> My dad always went with me the first trip or two because that was when the river was flowing ice and be freezing. So, there was always two of us that would go until the river froze up good. And then I carried it alone; well then I carried for the next three winters. (Biederman 1994: sec. 18)

The mail route was six days down and back with a rest day in between, thirteen trips a year, and four thousand miles a winter (Biederman 1994: sec. 19).

> Out of Eagle, we'd go down to Sheep Creek, Millers Wood Camp. He had a roadhouse there, Frank Miller. So, he had a bunkhouse there and place for us to put our dogs. So, we stayed there the first day. Next day we went down to Nation. At Nation we had our own cabin. First winter I

Ed and Bella Biederman. (Courtesy of Eagle Historical Society & Museums, EHS 056-0159-24.)

carried mail, well, Earl Stout, who later was in Central, he was there doing some prospecting. Then he worked Fourth of July as a miner in the summer. And he stayed in our cabin, so, of course, I stayed overnight with him because he ran it like a little roadhouse. I paid him so much a meal and so much a bed. Then next day [I'd] be at Charley Creek, mouth of Kandik. And we had our camp there, and there was an old Native guy who been around with us all our lives . . . Pat Dalfous. And he took care of our dogs, extra dogs, and then he had a little people coming through, paid him to stay there for the meals. So, he had a kind of little roadhouse. Then he trapped too. Then from Charley Creek, I went to Woodchopper. There was a Woodchopper roadhouse—that was Jack Walsh and his wife. They run that. That was a regular roadhouse because the people at Woodchopper and Cold Creek would come down there to pick up their mail and sometimes some of them would go to Circle or something. Well, they'd all stop over there just like a meeting place. They'd come down there to pick up their mail every two weeks, and so I would stop there. From there down to Circle, well, we built a cabin in the fall of 1935 on the south side [Twenty-Six Mile], so my dad and I went down there first trip on the mail, first two trips so he could stay there and finish up the cabin, put in the windows and the door, so he had it fixed up while I'd go on to Circle. Then, coming back, well, that year that's the only place I had to cook and heat the cabin up. There's nobody there. The second year, why, Earl Stout had left Nation, and I ended up there and same thing, warm the cabin up, cook for myself and do everything. So I had two places [to do everything]. Second winter, why, second winter I made a deal. We boarded with Fred Craiger at Nation. . . . Twenty-Six Mile, that was the only place where I had to take care of, cook for myself. (Biederman 1994: sec. 23)

That's how Biederman described the trail. For accommodations along the way, Biederman stayed at the Circle Roadhouse, where he got a meal for one dollar and a bed for a second dollar (Biederman 1994: sec. 24). Eagle old-timer Al Stout recalled Heine Miller saying to him: "The only one I'm happy to see coming is the mailman, and I'm glad when he's gone" (Stout 1991: sec. 3).

Charlie's final mail run took place in April 1938 (Skilbred 1998:18). By then, air service was in place. Some residents were concerned it might revert back to dog team delivery, and there were others who wanted the aviators to make stops along the way like the dog drivers used to do.[21]

Today, the Biederman sled, with iron runners and plow handles, sits on exhibit at the National Postal Museum in Washington, D.C. The sled is a tangible reminder of the hard miles of dog driving by the mail carriers on the Yukon ice.

The Trail Today

The trail is used each winter during the Yukon Quest sled dog race. There are trappers who use parts of the river corridor in winter.

EAGLE TO DAWSON

For thirty years, the primary mail carrier from Eagle to Dawson was Percy DeWolfe. He carried the mail from 1915 to 1950 and was seventy-three years old when he retired. He passed away less than a year later (Livermore 1977:17, 20).[22] This "iron man of the Yukon" (Livermore 1977) probably put in more years than any other dog team mail driver. When he retired in 1950, he was one of the last dog team mail carriers, rivaled only by Noongwook on St. Lawrence Island.

Percy DeWolfe, originally from Nova Scotia, came to the Yukon in 1898. He married Jessie Phillips and they had six children together (Livermore 1977:16; Scott 1997:108). Percy's run normally took four days: from Dawson, he would go to Halfway House (his home cabin), then on to Forty Mile, Midway Point, and finally into Eagle (Scott 1997:108). Each of these places was supplied in summer so he would be prepared for his winter runs with horses and dogs.

> On the Dawson-Eagle run, Percy DeWolfe, the contrac-
> tor, has been busy taking thirty tons of hay, oats, dog feed
> and groceries and the like down on his boat, the *Weasel*,
> and distributing them at Halfway House, Forty Mile,
> Midway Point, and Eagle. (Livermore 1997:18)

Charlie Biederman is shown here in Washington, D.C., at the time his sled was donated to the Smithsonian's National Postal Museum. (Photo courtesy of the National Postal Museum.)

Percy DeWolfe handing a sack of mail to RCMP constable Joe Kessler at Forty Mile. (Yukon Archives, Claude and Mary Tidd fonds, #7101.)

Claude Tidd, in the service of the Royal North West Mounted Police, got to know Percy over the years and was stationed on the mail run in the winter of 1937–38, probably at Forty Mile. With an eye for photography and a penchant for note taking, he left a record of the mail carrier:

> A few days after my talk with Percy, I saw him drive his sturdy team of eight huskies into the camp, every dog leaning into his collar and with his tail in the air as they lugged the heavily loaded sleigh up the steep bank. The thermometer that morning had registered forty below zero. Long before I could actually see him I could hear his cheery whistle and the familiar musical tinkle of the dog bells. I could even hear the crunch of his steel-shod sleigh runners on the frozen trail. In that still cold air all sounds carry very distinctly. As he came up the steep bank I could hear him urge his lead-dog "Mush Dempsey; mush on boy!" At the local Royal Canadian Mounted Police Post which also

All at work. Forty Mile, 1938. (Yukon Archives, Claude and Mary Tidd fonds, #7100.)

did duty as the Post-Office the dogs stopped and as the door opened and the bright light flooded the entrance I could see his burly caribou-skin-clad figure carrying in the sack of mail. In response to an inquiry from the uniformed figure of the lone Policeman "How's the trail to-day Percy?" I could hear his cheery voice boom in reply "Oh, not so bad; not so bad." (Tidd n.d.)

Things have changed a lot since Percy DeWolfe retired and the airplanes took over. Strangely enough, it takes a lot longer to get a letter from Dawson to Eagle. While researching for his book, *A Land Gone Lonesome*, Dan O'Neill sent a postcard from Dawson to Eagle to see how long it would take and compare the way things were done in the dog team days and how they are done today.

His postcard took ten days to go from Dawson to Eagle, traveling a distance of three thousand miles. Percy would have carried it one hundred miles in four days (O'Neill 2006:27) and probably with fewer

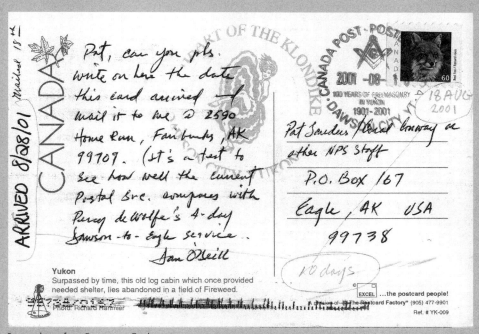

Postcard sent from Dawson to Eagle.

weather delays! Similarly, once it got to its destination, the carrier might have additional news to share from his stops on the trail, the added value that comes from traveling through the country.

The Trail Today

Percy DeWolfe's years of running the mail is commemorated in the annual Percy DeWolfe Memorial Mail Race from Dawson to Eagle and back.

six

The Aviators

The year is 1920 in the photograph that was hanging on Rose Zaverl's living-room wall. Rose's father, Bill Burk, is a young man in Signal Corps uniform, posing next to one of the Black Wolf Squadron planes in Ruby. Billy Mitchell had just commissioned the Black Wolf planes to fly across the United States and through the territory of Alaska, all the way to Nome on the Bering Sea coast. With his eye on aviation and the role it would someday play for the military (Cohen 1998), Billy Mitchell recognized the strategic importance of Alaska to the nation, and he advocated its development for defense (Cohen 1998:V).[1] Aviation had progressed substantially just seventeen years after the Wright Brothers, and, in the same manner as other early aviation feats, the Black Wolf squadron proved that aviation could be done in Alaska without familiar landmarks to follow. Billy Mitchell had first opened interior Alaska for overland commercial traffic with the telegraph line and was now signaling an even more significant change for the territory—flight over the country.

Bill Burk was sixteen when he came to Alaska from Illinois in 1905. At the time of the 1920 photograph, he had yet to carry mail via dog team on the Nenana to McGrath trail (Marie Allen, Bill Burk's daughter, pers. comm., May 26, 2006). Bill Burk may not have found this ironic, but it certainly illustrates both the inevitability and the elusive nature of aviation in Alaska. Aviation would become a natural fit for Alaska, but it would require tailoring to meet the unique conditions.

Aviation in interior Alaska went through several stages. There were demonstrations of the possibility of air travel, such as the 1924 Ben Eielson mail flight to McGrath. In the late 1920s, town groups and the Alaska Road Commission built airfields, while small airplane companies, such as Bennett-Rodebaugh Co., Inc., provided charter service to hunters and trappers.

Regularly scheduled service had to wait until advances in aviation: airfields, closed cockpits, weather reporting stations along the routes, radio systems for communication, and radial engines that replaced the earlier water-cooled models. The following chart illustrates the progression of aviation in the Interior.

SELECT CHRONOLOGY OF INTERIOR AVIATION

1913: James Martin flight in Fairbanks (Stirling 1982:2)

1920: Black Wolf Squadron flies New York City to Nome (Cohen 1998)

1922: Clarence Prest flies Juneau to Eagle; failed attempt to fly Eagle to Fairbanks (Tordoff 2002:29)

1923: Ben Eielson and Dick Wood fly Fairbanks to Nenana (Naske 1986:142)

1924: Noel Wien and Bill Yunker fly Anchorage to Fairbanks (Harkey 1974:77–83)

1924: Noel Wien flies Fairbanks to Wiseman (Stirling 1982:4)

1924: Ben Eielson flies mail Fairbanks to McGrath (Stirling 1982:3)

1925: Noel Wien flies Fairbanks to Nome (Naske 1986:142–143)

1928: Captain Hoyt flies Washington, D.C., to Nome (Waugaman 2007)

1928: Ben Eielson and Sir Hubert Wilkins fly Barrow to Spitsbergen, Norway (Mills and Phillips 1969:77)

1928: Alaska Road Commission reports fifteen airfields built for Fairbanks district (Naske 1986:145)

1931: Chart lists seventy-four airfields across Alaska territory (Naske 1986:146)

1932: Alaskan Airways planes have "modern" radial engines instead of old water-cooled engines (Tordoff 2002:169)

1932: Bob Gleeson hired by Pan American Airways to establish radio communication system (Tordoff 2002:177)

1932: Radio and weather station established at Fairbanks (Tordoff 2002:249)

1935: Radio and weather stations established at Burwash Landing, Juneau, McGrath, Nome, Nulato, Skagway, Taku, and Whitehorse (Tordoff 2002:249)

1936: Radio and weather stations established at Flat and Lake Minchumina (Tordoff 2002:249)

1938: U.S. Department of Interior reports 109 landing fields built in Alaska (Stirling 1982:11)

Bennett-Rodebaugh Co., Inc.

Airplane Service

Fairbanks, Alaska   **Chas. L. Thompson, Mgr.**

PASSENGER AND EXPRESS RATES--1928

Fairbanks to and from	One Pass.	Two or More Pass., Each	Express Per Lb.
Livengood	$ 50.00	$ 37.50	$ .15
Chena Hot Springs	50.00	40.00	.15
Nenana	50.00	40.00	.15
Palmer Creek	75.00	65.00	.20
Manley Hot Springs	100.00	80.00	.25
Circle Hot Springs	100.00	80.00	.25
Circle City	125.00	100.00	.30
Beaver	125.00	100.00	.30
Kantishna	125.00	100.00	.30
Minchumina	125.00	100.00	.30
American Creek	125.00	100.00	.30
Tanana	125.00	100.00	.30
Rampart	150.00	125.00	.40
Fort Yukon	150.00	125.00	.40
Bettles	175.00	137.50	.40
Wiseman	200.00	150.00	.40
Ruby	225.00	175.00	.50
Chandalar	225.00	175.00	.50
Eagle	225.00	175.00	.50
Tetlin Lake	250.00	200.00	.50
McGrath	250.00	200.00	.50
Tacotna	265.00	212.50	.50
Ophir	265.00	212.50	.50
Flat	300.00	250.00	.50
Iditarod	300.00	250.00	.50
Sleitmut	350.00	275.00	.75
Nulato	350.00	275.00	.75
Bethel	750.00	500.00	1.00
Nome	750.00	500.00	1.00
Kotzebue	750.00	500.00	1.00

BAGGAGE ALLOWANCE—20 Lbs. PER PASSENGER.
GOLD DUST AND FUR—DOUBLE EXPRESS RATE.
TRIPS BETWEEN INTERMEDIATE POINTS—$1.00 PER PASS. MILE.

Bennett Rodebaugh schedule 1928

There was a considerable period of overlap between the dog drivers and the aviators during the transition to airplane mail delivery. The aviators could carry the mail faster, and at what appears to be a lower cost per trip. However, this cost per trip does not account for the cost of purchase and maintenance of equipment, upkeep of aircraft, and work on the airfields.

There were other drawbacks. A chief complaint was that the airplanes could be held up by weather, whereas dog teams "always" got through.[2] Helge Boquist from Circle recalled that the dog team mail carriers used to bring the mail every week, but when Wien took over there were occasional weather delays, including one three-week period without mail (Boquist 1991: sec. 10).

Fred Thomas recalled that because bad weather affected the first year that planes started carrying the mail, dog teams took over again for the next couple of years (pers. comm., May 4, 2009). William Williams from Allakaket recalled that weather could hold up the mail, and the miners on the Upper Koyukuk would "squawk" if the mail didn't come through on time (Williams 1992: sec. 7). As mentioned, mail carrier Mike Cooney wanted to reestablish the dog team mail delivery trail system because of the unreliable airplanes he had been using between 1947 and 1949 (Mike Cooney to Alaska Road Commission, September 1949, State Department of Natural Resources RS 2477 file, "Nenana Route 1947–1950," Drawer 35). Historian Michael Brown wrote about the impact some residents felt:

> In 1933, some residents of the upper Kuskokwim basin circulated a petition, which was to be sent to the Alaska Delegate to Congress Anthony J. Dimond, for the reestablishment of the Nenana–McGrath trail as a winter mail route. The petitioners argued that the mail carriers, by keeping the trails open for travel, had played an important role in developing the country. Now that the mail service was suspended, trappers and prospectors were forced to abandon their businesses; the Indians, who had sold fish for dog feed were left without a means of livelihood; the prospectors and trappers along the trail did not receive mail for many months; and finally, all revenue received from the mail contracts was circulated in the district, which was not the case with the airline companies. (Brown 1980:89)

And there was the sign Sam White reported from a remote roadhouse:

> A big white sign with black letters I once saw at a remote roadhouse told the story. It read, "Aviator's trade not solicited here." (Rearden 2007:162)

There were, however, those who welcomed aviation and hoped it would provide better service. In a petition to the Postmaster General, some Eagle residents wrote:

> We have recently received information that there is a movement on foot, to put the mail contracts back with the Dog team Mail Contracters [contractors]. We sincerely hope such is not the case. Last winter there were forty days at one stretch we did not get any first class mail either by Dawson or from Fairbanks, until this winter mail has always been sure by Dawson. The dog team would come from Circle City sometimes with twenty pounds of mail. And two years ago they could not get the mail over Eagle Summit or only a small part of it between Fairbanks and Circle, always some excuse. (Eagle residents to Mr. James A. Farley, Postmaster General, June 9, 1938, National Archives Records)

By the late 1930s and the early 1940s, the aviators had taken over. The full impact of the transition was evident.

The airline companies provided cheaper service than the dog teams, but more was at stake than a simple economic equation. Direct flights segmented the land into village-focused units. With the end of the dog team mail carriers, many of the trails were abandoned. The winter connections between communities were broken, and the value of added news that the carriers brought from their stops along the trail was lost. Aviators brought news but they didn't spend time visiting unless they were delayed by weather or equipment. More often they were quickly in the air and on to the next stop.

seven

Homeland of the Old-Timers

Three days of overland travel by dog team from Fairbanks brought us to Tolovana, the historic roadhouse on the banks of the Tanana River. I stood with the roadhouse behind me, the river stretching out in front, lined with iron dog-trail markers. It was March, and the yearly long-distance snow machine race had just come through a few weeks before. The snow machine racers cover hundreds of miles in a day, and their sense of this place can't be anything more than a fleeting glance. Like the Iditarod and Yukon Quest dog team racers, they have their sights on the finish line—whatever is in between is of secondary consideration. When my thoughts turn back to the historic site behind me, I try to recapture a sense of this place when it was Charlie Shade's stop on the overland mail run, when it was the telegraph station, when it served the Athabaskans camped on the Tolovana River and the travelers making their way from Fairbanks to Manley and beyond. I think about the families who cut wood for the steamboats and fished for the dog teams; who trapped and hunted along the mail route and mined for gold farther downriver. Self-sufficiency and homegrown competence were the ingredients for a successful life in a country bountiful enough to support both local Natives and willing newcomers.

Elders may assume that young people today share a similar sense of this place and know the way certain landscapes look in the winter and what it took to get to and across them years ago. But many young people today grow up without knowing these places and without traveling much out on the land. They may have flown over prominent features mentioned in the elders' narratives, but they haven't been there on the ground. They don't have their own experiences of these places, the surrounding terrain, or a sense of the distances traveled by dog team.[1] Tim Ingold has captured this idea of movement through the country well: "Bound together by the itineraries of their inhabitants, places exist not in space but as nodes in a matrix of movement" (Ingold 2000:219, 230–231).

For Ingold, and the elders in this account, experiences in place and "journeying," the act of traveling through country, are the backdrop and context for historical knowledge of the places. Most of us don't have this same level of shared experience, so our understanding is of a secondary nature.

When the dog team mail carriers were definitively replaced by the aviators, we lost more than the trails: we lost a way of life represented by a generation that sustained and supported themselves on the land. Back then, travel depended on local knowledge, and local knowledge was critical to the

Tolovana Roadhouse, much as it looks today. (Photo courtesy of Kathy Lenniger.)

development of the country. Both the steamboat pilots and the dog team mail carriers depended on local knowledge of the water and the land, and this gave an advantage to people seasoned in the territory, particularly, although not exclusively, the Natives. Native river pilots held a privileged and unique position of responsibility, comparable in many ways to the dog team mail carriers, who were trusted with money, furs, and the post. In both cases, safe and dependable operation was based on skill in navigating the terrain and water bodies. For the mail carriers, the necessary knowledge also extended to their support system: the people who cared for the dogs and the women who made the winter clothing and dog booties, repaired harnesses, cut the fish to dry, and ran the roadhouses.

The trails in winter and the rivers in summer created a network of communication and a level of connection not seen today. The importance of this year-round network is illustrated in two historic events: the 1925 diphtheria epidemic and the sinking of the steamship *Sophia*.

The diphtheria epidemic of 1925 has become an important part of the oral and written tradition in Alaska (Salisbury and Salisbury 2003). When the epidemic struck in Nome, each dog team driver felt the seriousness of the situation and did his best to move the antitoxin along the trail from the Nenana railhead to Nome. The medicine and the story traveled through and gained life in the country. If the airplanes had won out and the serum had been flown to Nome, we might have had only one hero rather than twenty (Salisbury and Salisbury 2003:245). Without the participation of their families and neighbors, there would have been no role for the communities and camps along the way to share in the story.

Today, each serum runner is remembered for his role. The event gained national attention. The men who carried the serum gained fame, even though many of them, particularly the Natives, merely saw their accomplishment as part of the job they carried out routinely (Salisbury and Salisbury 2003:255; Donohoe 1980:91 quoting Edgar Kalland). Nationally, the drama of the race against time made for only half of the interest. The wild Alaska setting and the fact that dogs, as opposed to more modern forms of transport, made the heroic feat possible fascinated the nation. The national story focused on dangers, extreme winter weather, and the wildness of the country, but the drivers didn't consider the job unreasonable, the weather unusual, or the country wild. Travel could be dangerous, but this was their homeland (Berger 1988).[2] They were familiar with the country through travel, a level of competence honed by years of living there.

Taking the North Down with Her is the apt subtitle to Ken Coates and Bill Morrison's book, *The Sinking of the Princess Sophia* (Coates and Morrison 1991). The *Sophia*, on what was planned to be her last run of the season, sank off of Skagway in 1918. The passengers who lost their lives in that tragedy made up a cross section of northerners from interior Alaska and the Yukon on their way to Seattle. Many had made the trip by steamboat along the Tanana and Yukon. The steamboats had stopped in the villages and towns to pick up more passengers, drop off supplies for the winter, and take on wood for the boilers driving their large paddle wheels. By the time they reached Skagway, the passengers had visited with people in communities all along the river course. Coates and Morrison point out that the people in Alaska and the Yukon knew each other because they were connected by a transportation system extending through the country and linking communities. When the ship sank, the tragedy was felt throughout the territories (1991:xii).

The people and resources powering this economy and communication system were local. Those with trail and river skills were recognized for making the development of the North possible. These were the same people impacted financially when the airplanes came in, a point Sam White made in his story about the roadhouse sign refusing aviators' business. Sam knew both means of travel: he had worked the dog trails and stayed in the roadhouses before he took up flying, knowing the trails and the air routes both, so he was in a position to imagine the impacts aviation would have on the people who lived and worked along the trail system.

Today, aviation distances us from the land, and dog team transportation between villages is less than routine. The gap between the way things were done back then, in the days of the old-timers, and life today makes it difficult for many of us to understand that earlier era, the way people were related to the land and to each other. Today, most of us rarely travel far off the road system unless we're in an airplane, and our relationship to the country is different from that of the old-timers, who all traveled extensively on the land. Gaining perspective on the elders' sense of place is challenging. Fortunately, we have some clues in the way old-timers talk about their travels and their work on the land.

Their stories are about what happened, but the ways they remember and choose to talk about them are equally important: Todd Kozevnikoff's description of Donohue Lake where Jack Donohue lived, American Creek where the miners stayed, Fish Lake where Lester Erhart sent a message on the telegraph line. The elders' stories point to their personal connections to these places and their experiences of traveling between them. These clues help us begin to understand the historic settings, but without having shared in the experiences of the elders, we are left with an incomplete picture of what it was like.

This was particularly evident to me when I interviewed George O'Leary and Frank Warren. I was trying to understand their description of the mail route from Chatanika to Circle. They gave me a description that emphasized the natural features, captured in phrases like "down into the head of McManus Creek." Working from a map, I could follow their descriptions, but I realized that the route on the map wasn't a reflection of their knowledge of the country—what it actually meant to get "down into McManus Creek." They were actually traveling through their past experiences to reconstruct the landscape, whereas I was simply referencing lines on a map based on a mapmaker's representation of the country. My experience and understanding was a distant abstraction from their reality.

Of course, the cartographic record can spring to life when we make a personal connection to the record, when it becomes more than a representation of someone else's experience with space, and when someone else's experiences in a place have common points of comparison with our own experience. A year ago, I was thrilled to have a young trapper come visit me. He was interested in finding out about the trails around Purgatory, where he was trapping on his grandfather's line. As he pored over the handmade map by the Yanert brothers who lived there years ago, he linked the drainages, ridges, and trails to his experiences in the country. Hungry to know what the Yanerts experienced and how they lived, the trapper was fascinated by the old map because it related directly to his and his grandfather's sense of the land.

This spring, I had an experience with two seasoned woodsmen from Tanana that reminded me of the vital link between local travel and history. We were on Hay Slough—today the main winter overland route between Manley Hot Springs and Tanana—looking for holes in the river ice. The two men considered the old mail trail running parallel to the slough and surmised that it may have been less direct, but also less dangerous, than the slough, which is prone to spots of open water in winter. These men travel and work in the country, so they have the background to imagine, recognize, and appreciate the considerations of the old-timers who used the mail trail. This type of experience and knowledge and ability to relate to the earlier period is rare today, but it is vital to maintaining threads of continuity between the generations. Through their sense of the land and of local history, these men can reach back to the experiences of the elders in a direct way. Like the old-timers, they know and appreciate what it takes to travel and live in their homeland.

Acknowledgments

I want to recognize right up front Jack Coghill, who not only gave me the history of the trails out of Nenana but introduced me to Mae Speck, whose father, Charlie Shade, ran the mail. Rose Zaverl, originally from Nenana, was also very helpful about this section of the trail system. Her father, Bill Burk, ran the mail out toward McGrath. Todd Kozevnikoff gave a very personal account of traveling the mail trail between Tanana and Manley Hot Springs and the night they spent at the Manley Roadhouse. Bill Stroecker gave an account of his father, one of the earliest carriers on the Fairbanks trail, and he provided some key documents that he acquired from Rex Fisher.

Rex Fisher deserves special thanks in this publication for opening up his personal collection of newspaper and magazine clippings and sharing them with me. I have benefited from all of them and have referenced the following: *Fairbanks Daily News-Miner* 1937, *Fairbanks Weekly Times* 1908, *Dawson Yukon Sun* 1903, *Valdez News* 1901, *Fairbanks Daily Times* 1907, and the *Beaver* 1953. Rex's generous support extended to a detailed review of an early draft of this work.

On the Fairbanks to Circle trail, Frank and Mary Warren and Mary's brother George O'Leary were incredibly generous with their time, their knowledge of the trail, and their photographic collection. George did a mail run with his father at the end of the mail-carrying era. His father, Maurice O'Leary, is pictured on the cover of this work, a tribute to his years on one of the hardest trails of all. Ron Roman, youngest son of dog team mail carrier Walter Roman, shared his father's photographs of the trail and his early recollections of his dad. Grafton Bergman graciously allowed me to copy photographs of his father, Emil, when Emil was a mail carrier on the Rampart to Manley Hot Springs run and of Curly Wells who ran the mail from Circle to Fort Yukon. Bill Stevens shared a photograph of his father, John Stevens, who ran mail from Fort Yukon to Beaver and from Fort Yukon up the Porcupine River to the Canadian border. Louise Hutson allowed me to copy a photograph of her father, Kivik Riley, who ran the mail from Beaver up to Chandalar Lake. Thanks also to Michael Carey for supplying two great photos of Bill Burk. These personal connections with the mail carriers and the trails helped to keep this a local story based on what family and community members recall.

I received good support from people at the National Archives in Washington, D.C., the Yukon Archives in Whitehorse, the Pioneer Museum Archives at Pioneer Park in Fairbanks, the Eagle Museum in Eagle, the Anchorage Museum and Rasmuson Center in Anchorage, the Noel Wien Library in Fairbanks, and the Alaska State Library in Juneau. The RS 2477 records at the State Department of Natural Resources, now in Anchorage, were a helpful resource and particularly their set of U.S. Postal Service route maps. Talented graphic artist Dixon Jones created the three maps that provide overview and details of the country covered in the accounts. Dr. Patricia Holloway helped me with research on grasses native to the country and Richard Carroll Jr. provided a key source on the Circle–Fort Yukon trail.

Elisabeth Dabney, Taya Kitaysky, and Sue Mitchell worked patiently and skillfully to craft this manuscript into its final shape. Thank you!

Finally, I am thankful to the Alaska and Polar Regions Department at the University of Alaska Fairbanks for many of the images in this book.

Royalties from the sale of this book will go to the Alaska and Polar Regions Department in hopes that this may help in some small way to support the continued documentation and dissemination of knowledge about Alaska, the history, and the cultures that make this such a great place to live.

William Schneider
September 19, 2011

Notes

INTRODUCTION

1. My initial survey of the 1930 census reveals a complex picture of the population. Rampart, a mining town on the south bank of the Yukon, was the most interethnic of the communities I surveyed. Neighboring Manley Hot Springs appears to have been a predominantly white community. Fort Yukon, the largest of the communities surveyed, had a total population of 255 people with twelve listed as having both white and Native heritage. With the exception of Rampart, the census does not indicate a great deal of intermarriage. And so the mail carriers stand out as having participated in a high-status, contract-based activity that crosscut ethnic lines. This is unexpected for that time in history, considering that Alaska Natives' right to vote in Territorial elections did not become law until 1922; that it took two more years for the U.S. Congress to pass the Citizenship Act; and that it was 1945 before the Territorial legislature passed an anti-discrimination law. Yet the logbook for Knights Roadhouse on the Nenana to McGrath trail has entries for both Native and white mail carriers for 1926–1940, and my assumption is that these mail carriers were treated equally.

2. Kivik Riley's run was at the end of a chain of trails. He received the mail from the Fort Yukon driver, who received the mail from a driver coming from Circle. The mail reached Circle from Chatanika and reached Chatanika from Fairbanks, first on the Tanana Valley Railroad and then by the Steese Highway. The railroad began operation to Chatanika in 1907 and

continued until 1930 when the Steese Highway became the route of travel (Deely 1996:73, 141).

3. On a recent dog trip from Ester to Manley Hot Springs, I followed the old mail trail for most of the way. I camped at Tolovana near the old roadhouse in clear view of the Tanana River. I was reminded once again how easy it would be to think that the river was the mail carriers' highway and how important it was for me to reconstruct the historic overland routes.

CHAPTER ONE

1. While it is true that the U.S. military showed little interest in interior Alaska until the gold rush, there are a few notable exceptions. In 1869, responding to claims that the Hudson's Bay Company had not vacated their holdings after the U.S. purchase of Alaska, Captain Charles Raymond of the Engineer Corps was sent to determine whether there were foreign companies operating on American soil. His trip is noteworthy because he traveled on the first steamboat to ply the Yukon River, appropriately named the *Yukon* (Raymond 1900:34).

2. At this time, Indians were actively trading their furs at trading posts that catered to them and they were familiar if not already growing dependent on some food supplies from the posts. When the gold rushes hit, some Indians were impacted by less availability of supplies. Ray and Richardson reported this was the case for groups on the Porcupine River (Ray and Richardson 1900:551–552).

3. Schneider n.d.:6–7; Ray and Richardson 1900:530–531.

4. Ray to Adjutant General, U.S. Army, 15 September 1897, from Fort Yukon (Ray and Richardson 1900:527).

5. Ray's influence was immense, and his story is fascinating as well. He was a seasoned military man when he arrived on the Yukon. He had served in the Civil War and in the American West in the 1870s. From July 1881 to 1883, he was Commander of the International Polar Expedition to the Arctic Sea with the U.S. Signal Service. Ray twice sought reassignment to Alaska and finally was sent in August of 1897. Ray was reassigned to Cuba for about a year, and then, holding the rank of major, he returned to Alaska in charge of military affairs in the new district of North Alaska. In this capacity, he oversaw the exploration he had recommended from Cook Inlet and Prince William Sound as well as the construction of new military posts on the Yukon (Schneider n.d.:5). Fort Gibbon at Tanana and other military posts such as Fort Egbert at Eagle were quickly connected by a system of trails and a telegraph line that crisscrossed the Interior and changed the course of commerce. In the intervening years, 1898–1903, winter mail service was largely confined to the Yukon River corridor and from Dawson to the coast.

6. The contract was to carry the mail from Dawson to Fort Gibbon in 1898 (Simpson 1996). Downing had the Star Route to Nome from Dawson in 1899, where gold discoveries had prompted the demand and need for postal service (Andrews 1946).

CHAPTER TWO

1. The year 1880 is significant because this is when the Chilkoot Trail was open to prospectors and other non-Native travelers (Hanable 1978:323).
2. The White Pass and Yukon Route Company held many of the contracts in subsequent years until 1921, when other contractors—using horses, trucks, and tractors—took over.
3. Just three years later, the 1901 Postal Service map shows an established route from Valdez to Eagle, as well as the route Downing pioneered—Dawson to Eagle, Circle, and down the Yukon.
4. In a 1999 interview, Gulkana elder Fred Ewan told me that his grandfather, Chief Ewan, helped survey the route of the road from Glenallen or Copper Center up to around Sourdough (Ewan 1999). See also Ewan, 1999: sec. 7.)
5. The present Tolovana Roadhouse was restored by Doug Bowers in 1986 (Bowers and Bowers 2006). The 2008 spring flood severely damaged the structure, but it has been cleaned up since then.
6. While not shown on the map on p. 12, Charlie Campbell and Ruth Althoff believe they have found remnants of a telegraph line between Rampart and Tanana (pers. comm., December 9, 2008). This is consistent with the fact that there was a military presence at Rampart (Naske 1986:7) and that the purpose of the line was to connect the military installations. The line connecting Rampart and Tanana may have been completed after 1903.
7. Walker 2005:41.
8. In 1901, trader E.T. Barnette set up his post on the banks of the Chena River and met Felix Pedro, who would strike gold just one year later (Orth 1971:324; Cole 1991:36).
9. The 1905 Secretary of War report recognizes this route, noting Valdez to Copper Center, then from Copper Center to the mouth of the Big Delta River, and then from there down the Tanana to Fairbanks. The report goes on to say that twenty days or more could be saved over the existing delivery route that went from Skagway to Dawson, down the Yukon to Eagle trail, down the Eagle to Valdez trail, to the Fairbanks cutoff, and on to Fairbanks. The Secretary of War map for 1905 shows the entire trail from Valdez to Fairbanks. (U.S. Department of War 1905:299–315, map on 315; Fish 1905:61–62).
10. By 1905, Karstens and McGonagall were in the Kantishna mining district, where Karstens established what appears to be a private mail service (Walker 2005:22). The route most likely went to Nenana and then followed

the WAMCATS line from Nenana to Fairbanks (102). Karstens is well remembered and respected by Alaskans for his wilderness skills; he was a member of the successful 1913 climb of Denali, and in 1921 he became the first superintendent of Mt. McKinley National Park (204).

11. The trail that Stroecker and Date followed that winter likely took a shortcut from the WAMCATS line on the stretch from Ester to Old Minto. It probably headed west over a trail going from Fairbanks to Tolovana and Manley Hot Springs, as evidenced in the 1908–1914 Road Commission and 1914 Postal Service maps. While the maps show that this trail bypasses Minto, historian Claus Naske's description, and the logical direction path for the trail, follows Fairbanks to Ester, Dunbar, Minto, and finally to Manley Hot Springs. Dunbar was called Goldstream in the early years, and Minto is a reference to what is today called Old Minto. Naske notes that "The Nenana-Tanana, or Dunbar-Fort Gibbon winter bobsled road, formerly known as the Fairbanks-Ester-Fort Gibbon winter bobsled road, was the main winter route into all of western and northwestern Alaska" (Naske 1986:112). Further confirmation of the Goldstream to Minto cutoff comes from a 1907 newspaper article describing Fred Date and a crew cutting this trail ("Fred Date in with His Road Crew," *Fairbanks Daily Times*, December 6, 1907).

12. Bill, Stroecker's son, carried on in the banking business until his death in 2010. He was also an avid local historian who helped fill in some of the records in this work.

13. The sled road is mentioned in the 1908 Secretary of War report, but only shown as proposed on the 1905 map.

14. The trail north from Beaver to the gold mining activities in the Upper Koyukuk and at Chandalar Lake was known and used earlier. Turak Newman's accounts of travel and freighting on this route probably predates mail delivery (Newman n.d.). In the early years, winter mail service to the Upper Koyukuk communities was provided from Tanana. A route from Fort Gibbon (Tanana) went north to the Koyukuk River near Alatna and Allakaket and then farther upriver to Bettles, Coldfoot, Wiseman, and Nolan. This is shown on the 1914 and 1915 postal maps and may even predate this time, given that a trading post and post office were established at Bettles in 1899 and 1901, respectively (Couch 1957:20). This trading post served the mining interests that developed farther upriver at Coldfoot, Wiseman, and Nolan.

CHAPTER THREE

1. The discussion of horses and their role in delivery of mail and freight extends beyond the scope of this study and deserves a larger treatment. For instance, in my discussions with the Interior Alaska Trail Riders group in Fairbanks, members have been quick to point out the immense role horses played in transporting supplies into the Interior and their role in agriculture

before tractors became available. They have also pointed out that weather conditions made harvesting hay for horses problematic. Though grain was imported, there is some evidence that horses could survive primarily, if not exclusively, on native grasses—even in the winter (Andrews 1911:354; U.S. Department of Agriculture 1901:51). An examination of the hay harvests in the Tanana Valley may provide a better picture of the impact of poor growing seasons on the horse population and the eventual introduction of trucks and tractors. Pioneer geologist Alfred Hulse Brooks described native grasses as nourishing but notes that curing becomes a problem because of the early onset of frost. The frozen grasses don't have time to dry (Brooks 1953:408–409). Dr. Patricia Holloway, an agricultural specialist at the University of Alaska Fairbanks, had similar comments about the impact of fall rain or frost on the hay. She also made the point that the active growth cycle for the grasses ends early; the plants may look healthy, but they are pushing their nutrients into their roots. Horses grazing on these grasses late in the growing season won't be getting the nutrients they need (pers. comm., January 5, 2011).

In his study of the Valdez Trail, Kenneth Marsh argues that horse and automobile use temporarily overlapped on the Valdez Trail for two reasons: the volume of freight to be carried was greater than the motor vehicles could handle, and the horses were more reliable even though they were slower (Marsh 2008:374). Trucks eventually took over on the Richardson Highway, probably in the 1920s (Marsh 2008:373), and on the Steese Highway from Fairbanks to Circle, although the latter was largely closed to vehicle traffic in the winter (Ferguson 1998:H8–13). I do not know of any Native mail carriers who used horses, although there were a few Natives who used horses for freighting. Horse driving was introduced largely in response to the gold rushes, military exploration, road building, and telegraphic operations. Horses were critical for major freighting between large commercial centers, road construction, and agriculture. The tack was imported, and skilled workers made local repairs.

2. *Babiche* is moose hide cut in thin strips and soaked in water to make the hide pliable. The wet hide is used to tie the sled parts together. As the hide dries, it shrinks and provides a tight binding.
3. Richard Carroll Sr. told me that his father sold harnesses in his store in Fort Yukon. Jimmy Wells, whose father ran the mail in Fort Yukon, also noted that his dad bought dog collars (pers. comm., May 4, 2009).
4. Sammie Lennie of the Mackenzie Delta region recalled that his family made harnesses using wire pail handles, bent in a circle and stuffed with hair and wrapped with hide. Grant Spearman, who spent many years working with Nunamiut people in Anaktuvuk Pass, reports that the people in that region used to make dog collars by using bent willow, caribou fur, and canvas. He also documented an earlier style made from caribou hide with the hair left on for padding.

5. Dog booties are used to protect feet from moist snow that balls up in paws and causes cuts and bleeding. Rough ice can also damage paw pads, crippling dogs and making it difficult for them to work.

6. Yukon Archives hosts an amazing film of Percy DeWolfe starting off from Dawson on his run down to Eagle in the fall. Percy is shown rowing across the river with the mail sack just as the Yukon River is running ice. (Irving Snider film no. 3, V-44-3.)

7. For example, the Alaska Almanac for 1908 noted that the Northern Commercial Company reported holding the mail contracts for routes 78097 Tanana to Fairbanks, 78112 Circle to Cleary, 78111 Eagle to Tanana, 78113 Valdez to Fairbanks, and 78115 Fairbanks to Tanana.

8. In an article for the *Fairbanks Daily News-Miner*, Laurel Downing Bill noted that Clum became post office inspector for Alaska in 1898, traveling with his son all over the territory and parts of the Yukon and setting up post offices. Carrying mail sacks, keys, postal stamps, and dating and canceling stamps, he set Alaska up for government mail service ("Brave Men Blazed Alaska's Postal Trails," November 29, 2009, Sunday Edition, E1 and E3).

9. The Air Mail Act of 1925 "authorized the postmaster general to contract for domestic airmail service with commercial air carriers . . . set airmail rates and level of cash subsidies to be paid to companies that carried the mail." (U.S. Centennial of Flight Commission 1925).

10. Perhaps this is similar to our current challenges in combining Native ways of knowing with science. The two are difficult to reconcile because Native ways of knowing are based on a group's oral traditions and experience, while science is based on formulations applicable beyond the experience of a group and its traditions. According to Ong, scientific writing demands an objectivity that will produce universal conclusions outside the immediate experiment or event described (Ong 1982:113–114).

CHAPTER FOUR

1. Robert Charlie noted that the mail trail followed the river more closely than the existing trail (pers. comm., November 25, 2008). The Tanana River is notoriously dangerous, so the trail was overland with good reason.

2. According to Doug and Pete Bowers, the roadhouse was built by a man named Riley (Bowers and Bowers 2006).

3. Paul Esau's family was the last to leave Tolovana back in 1956–1957 (Paul Esau and Hank Ketzler, pers. comm., August 2, 2007).

4. The records of mail contracts in the National Archives aren't always reliable, but it is clear that Charlie Shade had the contract in 1934, 1938, 1942, and possibly in 1943. It would be fair to assume that he had the contract for the intervening years as well, since this is well within memory and Charlie is well known for carrying the mail on this trail.

5. Ambrose's son, Todd, told me that his dad moved up to Tanana from the St. Michael area and partnered up with his sister's husband, Edgar Kallands, to cut wood for steamboats (Kozevnikoff 2006). Edgar is remembered in the history books as one of the dog mushers who carried the diphtheria serum years earlier, when he was working for the Northern Commercial Company as an extra driver (Salisbury and Salisbury 2003:263). Edgar's dad was from Newfoundland and had the mail contract from Tanana to Nulato at one time; his mom, Angeline Titi, was from Nulato (Madison and Yarber 1982:12, 42). See also Bowers 1989:11–13.

6. Todd credited his grandfather's connection as a factor in his father's decision to work for the company carrying the mail (Virginia Kallands, daughter of Alex Kozevnikoff and wife of Edgar Kallands, pers. comm., November 15, 2006).

7. Some folks in Tanana remember the old mail trail and how it cut off some of the bad overflow as you get further up on Hay Slough. Of course, the lakes could pose their own problems with water, particularly in springtime.

8. I have rearranged and edited this quote to highlight Todd's trip.

9. National Archives records indicate that there was a contract for airplane service from Nenana to Tanana via Manley Hot Springs as early as 1931, and Edgar Kallands recalled in his biography that the airplanes started coming in 1932 (Madison and Yarber 1982:42). However, the postal records show that dog team mail contracts on this run continued until 1942. The overlap is mysterious, but there are other cases of overlapping air and dog team service. A recurring theme throughout the records is how long it took to get dependable scheduled air service.

10. Allakaket and Alatna elders Moses Henzie, Joe Beetus, and William and Effie Williams remember Andrew Kokrine and his boys (Tony, Bergman, and Andrew Jr.). William Williams from the Upper Koyukuk recalled that Andrew's boys would often be along to break trail for him on snowshoes (pers. comm., August 6, 2009).

11. The archival record for this route is spotty, showing only three years: a 1918 contract going to the Northern Commercial Company for Manley to Tanana, Bettles, Coldfoot, and Nolan; a 1922 contract to a John Adams for the same route; and a 1931 contract to Alaska Airways for Tanana to Alatna, Bettles, and Wiseman.

12. Johnny Adams is probably the same man who married Episcopal Deaconess Mabel Pick, who was stationed at Tanana in 1922 (Fredson 1922:139–141).

13. Margaret's parents were from Nuklukayet (Tanana), where her father was a chief (see also Haigh 1996:45–48). The National Archives holds Emil's 1922 contract and Alfred Woods's 1926 contract.

14. Elsie Lasiter of Rampart also mentioned Tommy Evans as the last one to carry the mail before the airplanes took over. Tommy's son, Ronnie Evans, also confirmed that his father carried the mail and mentioned that his

grandfather, John Williams, may have as well (pers. comm., March 16, 2010).

15. Phyllis Downing Carlson and Laurel Downing Bill report that the last "official" dog team mail contract on this run was for 1949 (Carlson and Bill 2007:185).

16. Moses Paul told me that Mike had his house down by the *Taku Chief*, the old riverboat that sits alongside the highway today. He remembered that when he was a young boy, he helped the mail carrier hook up his big string of dogs (Moses Paul, pers. comm., August 2, 2007). Howard Luke told me that Mike once had such a big load, he used three sleds tied together.

17. Jack refers to the postmaster as "Elsie," but in a postal history he is referenced as Lauritz C. Olson (Couch 1957:37). Mike has contract records for 1934, 1938, 1942, and 1946.

18. The Knights Roadhouse logbook is located at the Pioneer Museum archival collection at Alaskaland (Pioneer Park) in Fairbanks, Alaska.

19. The trail had several sections. Some of the carriers worked farther out the line and are not reflected in this diagram but will be discussed. Some carriers also moved up and down the line as demand warranted, so they could be carrying mail and not staying at this site.

20. Rose Zaverl, Bill Burk's daughter, said that her dad worked for the Army Signal Corps Service before marrying a woman named Rose Big Joe from the Ruby area in 1922 (pers. comm.)

21. For further reference to the roadhouse, see August and September letters from Bobby Esai, Leo Keogh interview notes with Dianne Gudgel-Holmes (June 14, 1983, Anchorage Consortium Library Archive), and Brown 1980:87.

22. Lars Nelson appears in the Knights Roadhouse log and is reported by Judge Clegg on the run between Lonestar Roadhouse and Big River in 1928 (*Fairbanks Daily News-Miner*, February 6, 1928). According to his 1941 obituary, he died of silicosis at the age of fifty, having spent many of his thirty years in Alaska as a mail carrier on the Nenana to McGrath trail (Obituary for Lars Nelson, *Fairbanks Daily News-Miner*, May 17, 1941). Miska Deaphon's life as a mail carrier is described briefly in Pulu 1975:8 and also referenced in an *Alaska Native Magazine* video (*Alaska Native Magazine* film 1975).

23. Mike Brown reported that the 1923 post office contract to Ben Eielson was for ten weeks of weekly flights, and the first flight was on February 21, 1924 (Brown 1980:100; see also Potter 1947). In the 1975 *Nikolai Reader*, Miska Deaphon reported hearing the rattling while hunting moose toward Telida; he was frightened (Pulu 1975:5). Miska also reported serving as a mail carrier in 1930 and 1931 (*Alaska Native Magazine* film 1975). He used twenty-one dogs to carry the mail between Lonestar Roadhouse and Big River, and it took him three days each way at fifteen dollars a day. He reported that the airplanes took over that run in 1932 (Pulu 1975:8).

24. Perhaps this is similar to the towns that supplied fuel and water for steam locomotives traveling the rail lines across the country. Many of those towns disappeared when the trains switched over to diesel.
25. The early aviators in the continental U.S. followed railroad lines. By 1923, there were airline beacons across part of the country (Schwantes 2003:193, 200).

CHAPTER FIVE

1. Both Sergi Cherosky and Pitka Pavaloff were half Russian and half Athabaskan. Pitka's sister, Erina Pavaloff Cherosky Callahan, recounted that after they found gold at what they called "Pitka Bar" on Birch Creek, Pitka and Sergi floated down to Tanana and then went upriver by steamboat to Forty Mile to get an outfit. When they headed back down to their find on Birch Creek, they were followed by other prospectors (Brooks 1953:328).
2. Reporting in 1897, the U.S. Geological Survey geologist Harold Goodrich noted that Natives were not permitted to hold claims (Goodrich 1898:120–121). Most Natives were not given the rights of citizenship, a legal point stemming from the Treaty of Cession with Russia, and therefore it was claimed they had no legal rights. Underlying the legal issue was the attitude of some miners that Natives were unreliable. For further explanation, see Schneider 1986:161–162.
3. The Fairbanks to Chatanika section of rail line was completed in 1907 and was in operation until 1930, a year after the Steese Highway connected Fairbanks and Circle by road. Later, the highway made train service unprofitable, and the road become the main summer route for hauling supplies to the mining camps (Deely 1996:73, 140–141). After its completion in 1930, the mail carriers used a combination of road and trail, trucks and dog teams in the wintertime.
4. Palm was recorded as the carrier in 1920 in the *Fairbanks Daily News-Miner*. Palm arrived in Fairbanks on the train from Chatanika with two hundred fifty pounds of first-class mail that had been offloaded from the *Hazel B*, a river launch ("First Class Mail Arrives," October 19, 1920).
5. The earliest record I have found is from 1914: "John Palm and Jules Marion will leave for Chatanika in two days to open the mail route between Chatanika and Circle. They are the only carriers and will make alternate trips" (*Fairbanks Daily News-Miner* 1989).
6. Maurice O'Leary also froze his hands hauling the mail with horses and had to have some fingers amputated (Mary and Frank Warren, pers. comm., July 15, 2010).
7. Horse-drawn stages and sleds serviced the Valdez to Fairbanks trail that later became the Richardson Highway. Horses held out on that route until carriers began using motorized vehicles. In many other places, despite road

construction and the early use of horses, dogs proved to be a better way to carry the mail. As roadhouses closed down, it became harder to maintain horses on the routes.

8.   Starting from the Circle end, the old trail followed the foothills north of the existing road to Birch Creek. It crossed the creek and continued on the higher ground until a few miles out of Central, where it dropped down into the community. Then it followed mostly the existing road to Mammoth and Miller Creeks, went up Miller and over the summit to Eagle Creek, down to Ptarmigan, and on to the mouth of Fish Creek. From there, it followed the Birch Creek drainage to Twelve Mile Creek. The trail went up Twelve Mile Creek and "over the hill" into McManus Creek. From there it went down to the Chatanika River and on to the settlement at Chatanika (Warren and O'Leary 2008).

There were other dog team mail carriers on this route but we know the most about the O'Learys, Walter Roman, Walter Jewell, and Johnny Palm (Ferguson 1998:H11). Jane Williams recalled Johnny Lake running the mail to Miller House until Jerry Rivard took over with his truck and car (Williams 1995). Charlie Biederman recalled a Bert Thornsen on the Chatanika to Circle run as well (Skilbred 1998:12).

9.   Both Jimmy Wells and Fred Thomas remember Rooster (pers. comm., May 4, 2009). Joe Herbert, who lives in Chalkyitsik, also recalls Curly's loose leader coming to the post office in Fort Yukon (pers. comm., September 9, 2009).

10.   The mail trail ran mostly off the south bank of the Yukon. Out of Fort Yukon, it headed upriver to Seventeen Mile, then inland. The first stop would be at forty-five miles below Circle. Then he would go on to Half Way Cabin, then Twenty-One Mile Cabin, and the next day he would reach Circle (Jimmy Wells, pers. comm., May 4, 2009).

11.   Charlie Biederman reported that Curly's son, Arthur, did the winter runs in 1934–35 and 1935–36 (Skilbred 1998:12).

12.   Located in the Postal Services Search File at the Yukon Archives in Whitehorse. I suspect it is from a Vancouver paper.

13.   John Stevens was married to Maggie, originally from Mayo, who worked at the hospital in Fort Yukon (Bill Stevens, pers. comm., October 5, 2006). Big Steve was married to Charlotte. John Stevens and Steven John were partners (Fred Thomas, pers. comm., October 4, 2006; Clarence Alexander, pers. comm., May 5, 2009; Richard Carroll Sr., pers. comm., May 4, 2009).

14.   The National Archives shows postal contracts with Riley for 1931, 1934, and 1938–1942 (National Archives RG28).

15.   Frank Yasuda was the trader in Beaver. When the airplanes took over, Kivik Riley came to town and worked on the road and then for the railroad. He died in 1980 at the age of eighty-one or eighty-two.

16. Others who are remembered as mail carriers on this route are Art James, Percy Herbert, and Pete Wallis (Fred Thomas, pers. comm., October 4, 2006; Richard Carroll Sr., pers. comm., January 30, 2007).

17. Clarance recalls that he was a big, 250-pound man, "all muscle." Richard Martin described traveling with Big Steve on the mail trail in 1928 (Martin 1993:1–6). Sam White also mentions meeting Big Steve (Rearden 2007:103).

18. The Fort Yukon to New Rampart route does not appear on the 1924 postal map. However, it is on the 1931, 1932, 1937, 1938, and 1940 maps, showing the Fort Yukon to Rampart House trip taken three times a year. An airplane symbol on the 1943 postal map indicates the transition to air service.

19. In an interview with Laurel Tyrell, Charlie Biederman claims that his father started on this run in 1910 (Biederman 1994: sec. 2). Skilbred also makes this claim (1998:4–5). O'Neill (2006:158), Scott (1997:102), and Webb (1977) indicate that Ed Biederman started on this run in 1912.

20. The primary sources for the chronology are Skilbred (1998), Scott (1997), Webb (1977), Webb (1985), and O'Neill (2006). As mentioned above, there is disagreement as to whether Ed started carrying the mail in 1910 or 1912. All agree that Ed Biederman froze his feet in 1925 and that his son Horace took over, but it is unclear if Horace took over right away. All sources agree that Charlie Biederman was the last dog team mail carrier on this route, giving way to the airplanes at the end of the 1938 season.

21. Two letters in the National Archive files point to different issues surrounding the transition, one voicing concern that the mail service not revert back to dog teams (Farley to Postmaster General, June 9, 1938), the other calling for a mail stop by airplanes at Charlie Creek (Beck to Chief Railroad Mail Clerk, September 3, 1941).

22. See Scott (1997:109) and O'Neill (2006:26) for confirmation that DeWolfe lost the contract to airmail in 1951.

CHAPTER SIX

1. The Black Wolf Squadron's official name was the Alaska Flying Expedition, and this flight was Billy Mitchell's brainchild.

2. Despite the common lore, "always" is too strong a word to express the punctuality of dog team mail delivery.

CHAPTER SEVEN

1. In some respects this is similar to the issues described by Ken Ryden in his book *Mapping the Invisible Landscape* (1993). In the opening chapter, Ryden describes the evolution of roads from trails to interstates and the difficulties of uncovering and understanding the way the land was

used during each stage of its evolution. The difference is that the country Ryden describes has been continuously traveled, albeit in different ways, unlike vast stretches of interior Alaska that now see few travelers.

2. The title of Thomas Berger's book, *Northern Frontier, Northern Homeland* (1988), captures the difference between those who see the North as a new country, foreign and dangerous, a place to be explored for what it can offer, and those who view it as a homeland, a familiar place with a population of people with shared experiences and traditions.

Bibliography

Note: OHC citations refer to the collection at the Alaska and Polar Regions Department, Rasmuson Library, University of Alaska Fairbanks.

Alaska Almanac. 1908. Seattle: Harrison Publishing Company.

Alaska Department of Natural Resources. 1949. R.S. 2477 file, "Nenana Route 1947–1950," drawer 35. Letter from Mike Cooney to Alaska Road Commission, Sept. 29.

Alaska Native Magazine #3 (film). 1975. University of Alaska Fairbanks, Alaska and Polar Regions Archives, Alaska Archival Film (AAF) 5879.

Alaska Road Commission. 1915. *Report of the Board of Road Commissioners for Alaska, 1915.* Washington, D.C.: Government Printing Office.

———. 1929. *Annual Report of the Alaska Road Commission, Fiscal Year 1929. Report Upon the Construction and Maintenance of Military and Post Roads, Bridges, and Trails; and of Other Roads, Tramways, Ferries, Bridges, Trails, and Related Works in the Territory of Alaska.* Juneau: Board of Road Commissioners for Alaska.

Allen, Henry. 1900. "A Military Reconnaissance of the Copper River Valley, 1885." *Compilation of Narratives of Exploration in Alaska.* Washington, D.C.: Government Printing Office. 411–488.

Andrews, C. L. 1911. "Agriculture in Alaska." *Alaska-Yukon Magazine* 12: 352–356.

———. 1946. "Ben Downing: Pioneer and Frontiersman." *Alaska Life*, February, p. 15–18.

Attla, Catherine. N.d. Oral history recording, OHC, H2000-33-01 and H2000-33-02.

Baird, A. 1953. "Yukon Postal Service." *Dawson Weekly News*, May 28. Postal Collection, Yukon Archives.

Barnhardt, Carol. 1985. *Historical Status of Elementary Schools in Rural Alaskan Communities, 1867–1980*. Fairbanks: Center for Cross-Cultural Studies, University of Alaska Fairbanks.

Beetus, Joe. 1996 & 2004. Oral history interviews with Mike Spindler and Orville Huntington (interviewers) for Raven Radio. OHC, H2004-01-27 (see also Raven Story Jukebox, Joe Beetus, sec. 3). http://jukebox.uaf.edu/RavenStory/htm/jcb.htm.

Berger, Thomas. 1988. *Northern Frontier, Northern Homeland: The Report of the MacKenzie Valley Pipeline Inquiry*. Toronto: James Lorimer & Co. Vol. I and II.

Bertoson, Gordon. 1991. Yukon-Charley Rivers National Preserve Project Jukebox, OHC, H91-22-53 and H91-22-54. http://jukebox.uaf.edu/YUCH/htm/gordon.htm.

Biederman, Charlie. 1994. Central Reflections, Then and Now Project Jukebox, OHC, H95-14. http://jukebox.uaf.edu/central/biohtm/chbib.html.

Biederman, Horace. 1965. Oral recording from Tanana-Yukon Historical Society talk. OHC, H97-66-11.

Bill, Laurel Downing. 2009. "Brave Men Blazed Alaska's Postal Trails." *Fairbanks Daily News-Miner*. November 29. Sunday edition E1 & E3.

Boquist, Helge. 1991. Yukon-Charley Rivers National Preserve Project Jukebox, OHC, H91-22-50. http://jukebox.uaf.edu/YUCH/htm/boquist.htm.

Bowers, Peter. 1989. "Edgar Kallands' Serum Run." *Mushing Magazine* (December/January): 11–13.

Bowers, Peter, and Doug Bowers. 2006. OHC, H2006-19.

Brooks, Alfred Hulse. 1953. *Blazing Alaska's Trails*. Fairbanks: University of Alaska and Arctic Institute of North America.

Brown, Cary. 1986. "Circle to Eagle Historic Trail: An Overview." Historic Mail Trail, Yukon-Charley Rivers National Preserve. Resource Management Library. Fairbanks: National Park Service files.

Brown, Michael. 1980. "Navigable and Nonnavigable Waters in the Upper Kuskokwim River Basin." Report to Chief, Division of Resources, through the Chief, Branch of Lands and Minerals, Bureau of Land Management.

Brown, Walter F. 1929. Advertisement Inviting Proposals for Carrying the Mails of the United States on the Steamboat or Other Power-Boat Routes and the Star Routes in the Territory of Alaska from July 1, 1930, to June 30, 1934. Washington, D.C.: U.S. Government Printing Office (Alaska Commercial Company collection, Department of Special Collections, Stanford University Libraries, JL006, box 13, folder 3).

Callahan, Erinia Pavaloff Cherosky. 1975. "A Yukon Autobiography." *Alaska Journal* 5(2): 127–128.

Campbell, Colin. 1902. *The White Pass & Yukon Route to the Golden North*. Seattle: Press of the Trade Register.

Carlson, Phyllis Downing, and Laurel Downing Bill. 2007. *Aunt Phil's Trunk, An Alaskan Historian's Collection of Treasured Tales*, vol. 2. Anchorage: Laudon Enterprises.

Carroll, James. 1957. *The First Ten Years in Alaska: Memoirs of a Fort Yukon Trapper, 1911–1922*. New York: Exposition Press.

Cavagnol, Joseph. 1957. *Postmarked Alaska: A Saga of the Early Alaska Mails*. Holton: Gossip Printery.

Clum, John P. 1910. "Alaska's Postal Service." *The Valdez-Fairbanks Trail, Alaska*. Compiled by Hallock C. Bundy. Seattle: Alaska Publishing Company. 65.

Coates, Ken, and Bill Morrison. 1991. *The Sinking of the Princess Sophia: Taking the North Down with Her*. Fairbanks: University of Alaska Press.

Cody, H. A. 1908. "Alaska-Yukon Overland Mail: Past and Present." *Pacific Monthly* 20 (December): 641–648.

Coghill, Jack. 1995. Fairbanks Communities of Memory Project Jukebox, OHC, H2008-04-01. http://jukebox.uaf.edu/comfbks/Coghill_Jack1/HTML/testimonybrowser.html.

———. 2004. Oral history interview with Terrence Cole (interviewer). OHC, H2005-01-16, pt.2.

———. 2006. Oral history interview with William Schneider (interviewer). OHC, H2006-10.

Cohen, Stan. 1998. *The Alaska Flying Expedition: The U.S. Army's 1920 New York to Nome Flight*. Missoula: Pictorial Histories Publishing Company.

Cole, Terrence. 1991. *Crooked Past: The History of a Frontier Mining Camp: Fairbanks, Alaska*. Fairbanks: University of Alaska Press.

Couch, James. 1957. *Philately Below Zero; A Postal History of Alaska*. State College, PA: American Philatelic Society.

Cribbens, Norman. 1940. "City Man Carried U.S. Mail in North." Postal Services Search File, Yukon Archives, Whitehorse, Yukon Territories, Canada.

Cruikshank, Moses. 1986. *The Life I've Been Living*. Fairbanks: University of Alaska Press.

Dawson Yukon Sun. 1903. "Will Mark the Trail to Eagle; Ben Downing Will Lay Out Trail with View of Making It as Straight as Possible." Nov. 14, p. 4. (Rex Fisher collection.)

Deely, Nicholas. 1996. *Tanana Valley Railroad, the Gold Dust Line*. Fairbanks: Denali Designs.

Department of the Interior. 1975. "Alaska Gold Rush Trails Study: Koyukuk-Chandalar Routes Preliminary Draft." Department of the Interior, Bureau of Outdoor Recreation.

Dogs of the North. 1987. *Alaska Geographic* 14, no. 1.

Donohoe, Mathew. 1980. "All in a Day's Work." *Alaska Magazine* xlvi, no. 3 (March): 16–21, 91–94.

Doogan, Mike. 1988. *Dawson City.* Anchorage: Alaska Geographic Society 15(2).

Edwin, Lee, and Teddy Luke. N.d. Oral history interview. OHC, H78-184.

Episcopal Church. 1896. "Domestic Missions: Mail Carrying in Alaska." *The Spirit of Missions.* New York: Domestic and Foreign Missionary Society. 265–268.

Ewan, Fred. 1999. Wrangell-St. Elias National Park Project Jukebox, OHC, H99-25. http://jukebox.uaf.edu/WRST/gulkana/gul.htm.

Fairbanks Daily News-Miner. 1916. "All the Mail All the Time Urged by Deal." Sept. 9, p. 3.

———. 1920. "First Class Mail Arrives." Oct. 19, p. 2.

———. 1928. "Four Naturalized at McGrath Term." Feb. 6, p. 8.

———. 1937. "Dog Teams Mush Mail For Circle." December 18, p. 9. (Rex Fisher collection.)

———. 1941. "Miner Dies Here After Long Illness; Lars Nelson Called Victim of Silicosis, Dread Miners' Disease." May 17, p. 4.

———. 1953a. "John Palm, 87, Dies in Seattle Thursday." June 2, p. 7.

———. 1953b. "John Palm's Ashes Scattered over Old Mail Route." June 10, p. 1.

———. 1989. "Looking Back, 75 Years Ago: Oct. 29, 1914." October 29, p. A2.

———. 2005. "Early Alaska Postal Service Was Rough Business." Dec. 11, p. E1, E10.

Fairbanks Daily Times. 1907. "Fred Date in With His Road Crew." Dec. 6, p. 4. (Rex Fisher collection.)

Fairbanks North Star Borough. 1981. Fairbanks North Star Borough Inventory of Historic and Recreational Trails, October 1981.

Fairbanks Weekly Times. 1908. "H. Schaupp of Little Eldorado in Town." December 5. (Rex Fisher collection.)

Farnsworth Family Papers. 1887–1911. Box 1, folder 3, p. 44. Alaska and Polar Regions, Elmer E. Rasmuson Library, University of Alaska Fairbanks.

Ferguson, Judy. 1998. "By Dog, by Horse, by Truck: Carrying Their Load, Early Mail Handlers Found the Will and the Way." *Heartland Magazine*, February 8. H8–14.

Ferrell, Ed, ed. 1994. *Biographies of Alaska-Yukon Pioneers 1850–1950.* Westminster, MD: Heritage Books.

Fish, James. 1905. "Alaska's Mail and Telegraph Service." *Alaska Magazine* 1 (April): 61–62.

Francis, Bella. 1993. Oral history interview with Roger Kaye. OHC, H94-37-01.

Frank, Richard. 1991. Oral history interview with William Schneider and Malinda Chase (interviewers). OHC, H92-09.

Fredson, John. 1922. "The First Cruise of Pelican II." *Alaska Churchman* no. 4: 139–141.

Galbraith, Betty, and William Galbraith. 1976. *Core Alaska Newspapers: 1866–1970.* Denver: self-published.

"Glimpses of Life in the Yukon: 100,000 miles with a Dog Team." MSS61, 77/19, File 2 of 2. Claude Britiff Tidd Collection, Yukon Archives. Pp. 6–7.

Goodrich, Harold. 1898. "History and Condition of the Yukon Gold District to 1897." Pp. 103–133 in *Geology of the Yukon Gold District, Alaska*. Josiah Edward Spurr. U.S. Geological Survey, 18th Annual Report. Washington, D.C.: Government Printing Office.

Haigh, Jane. 1996. "...And his Native wife." *Preserving and Interpreting Cultural Change*. Proceedings of the Alaska Historical Society Annual Meeting, 1996. 39–54.

Hales, David. 1980. *An Index to the Early History of Alaska as Reported in the 1903–1907 Fairbanks Newspapers*. Elmer E. Rasmuson Library Occasional Papers, no. 8. Fairbanks: Elmer E. Rasmuson Library, University of Alaska Fairbanks.

Hall, Edwin. 1978. "Technological Change in Northern Alaska." *Archaeological Essays in Honor of Irving B. Rouse*. Robert C. Dunnell and Edwin S. Hall, Jr. The Hague: Mouton Publishers. 209–229.

Hanable, William. 1978. "When Quarterdeck Was Capital." *Alaska Journal* 8, no. 4: 320–325.

Harkey, Ira. 1974. *Noel Wien: Alaska Pioneer Bush Pilot*. Fairbanks: University of Alaska Press.

Henkin, David. 2006. *The Postal Age: The Emergence of Modern Communications in Nineteenth-Century America*. Chicago: University of Chicago Press.

Hudson, Sally. 1985. Oral history recording for Elders in Residence class at University of Alaska Fairbanks. OHC, H90-06-97.

Ingold, Tim. 2000. *The Perception of the Environment: Essays on Livelihood, Dwelling, and Skill*. London: Routledge.

Kimball, Frank. 1912. "Alaska's Mail Service." *Overland Monthly* LIX, no. 4: 293–297.

Kokrine, Effie. 1987. Oral history interview with William Schneider, Sue Will, and Doris Southall (interviewers). OHC, H87-16.

Kozevnikoff, Wilfred (Todd). 2006. Oral history interview with William Schneider. OHC, H2006-27.

Livermore, Carol. 1977. "Percy DeWolfe, 'Iron Man of the Yukon.'" *The Beaver* (Autumn): 16–20.

Lowe, P. G. 1900. Sub-report of "A military reconnaissance of the Copper River Valley, 1898." *Compilation of Narratives of Explorations in Alaska*. Washington, D.C.: Government Printing Office. 591–593.

MacBride, William D. 1953. "Yukon Stage Line." *The Beaver* (June): 43–45. (Rex Fisher collection.)

Madison, Curt, and Yvonne Yarber. 1982. *Edgar Kallands, Kaltag: A Biography*. Fairbanks: Spirit Mountain Press.

Marsh, Kenneth. 2008. *The Trail: The Story of the Historic Valdez-Fairbanks Trail That Opened Alaska's Vast Interior*. Trapper Creek, AK: Trapper Creek Museum.

Martin, Richard (as told to Bill Pfisterer). 1993. *K'aiiroondak: Behind the Willows*. Fairbanks: University of Alaska Fairbanks.

Mason, Michael. 1934. *The Arctic Forests*. London: Hodder and Stoughton, Ltd.

McKennan, Robert A. 1959. *The Upper Tanana Indians*. Yale University Publications in Anthropology no. 55. New Haven: Department of Anthropology, Yale University.

———. 1981. "Tanana." Pp. 562–576 in *Handbook of North American Indians: vol. 6, Subarctic*. Edited by June Helm. Washington, D.C.: Smithsonian Institution.

McLain, John Scudder. 1905. *Alaska and the Klondike*. New York: McClure, Phillips & Co.

McLean, Dora. 1963. "Early Newspapers on the Upper Yukon Watershed: 1894–1907." Master's thesis. University of Alaska Fairbanks.

Mercier, François Xavier. 1986. *Recollections of the Youkon: Memories from the Years 1868–1885*. Anchorage: Alaska Historical Society.

Michael, Henry, ed. 1967. *Lieutenant Zagoskin's Travels in Russian America, 1842–1844*. Toronto: Arctic Institute of North America, University of Toronto Press.

Mills, Stephen, and James Phillips. 1969. *Sourdough Sky: A Pictorial History of Flights and Flyers in the Bush Country*. Seattle: Superior Publishing Company.

Mitchell, William L. 1982. *The Opening of Alaska*. Lyman Woodman, ed. Anchorage: Cook Inlet Historical Society.

Murie, Margaret. 1997. *Two in the Far North*. Anchorage: Alaska Northwest Publishing. Reprint.

Murray, Alexander Hunter. 1910. *Journal of the Yukon, 1847–48*. Ottawa: Publication of the Canadian Archives, no. 4. Government Printing Office.

Naske, Claus. 1986. *Paving Alaska's Trails: The Work of the Alaska Road Commission*. Alaska Historical Commission Studies in History, no. 152. Lanham, MD: University Press of America.

National Archives, Washington, D.C. Records from the office of the Second Assistant Postmaster General, Division of Surface Postal Transportation, Alaska Main Service, contract case files RG 28 and 29, boxes 8, 9, and 10.

———. 1943. Charles Shade to Chief Clerk Earl L. March, District no. 6, Railway Mail Service, Anchorage, Alaska. Oct. 20.

———. 1945. Chief Clerk of the Railway Mail Service to Smith Purdum, second assistant postmaster general, Railway Mail Service. Sept. 10.

———. 1942. Jesse Evans to the second assistant postmaster general, Railway Mail Service, received by Division of Railway Adjustments. April 25.

———. 1938. 16 Eagle Residents to James A. Farley, postmaster general. June 9.

———. 1941. George Beck to chief railroad mail clerk, Seward, Alaska. Sept. 3.

National Park Service. N.d. "Yukon-Charley Rivers Preserve Historic Sites." National Park Service. http://www.nps.gov/yuch/historyculture/historic-sites.htm/index.htm.

Nelson, Barbara. 1995. Rampart Picture History: A Photo Jukebox, Alaska and Polar Regions, Elmer E. Rasmuson Library, University of Alaska Fairbanks. http://jukebox.uaf.edu/Rampart/html/mayon.htm.

Nelson, Jerry. 1997. "Perils of the Trail: Tales of Early Alaska and Yukon Mail Carriers." *Mushing* no. 54: 27–28, 30.

Newman, Turak. N.d. *One Man's Trail*. Anchorage: Adult Literacy Laboratory.

O'Neill, Daniel. 2006. *A Land Gone Lonesome*. New York: Counterpoint Press.

Ong, Walter. 1982. *Orality and Literacy: The Technologizing of the Word*. London: Methuen.

Orth, Donald. 1971. *Dictionary of Alaska Place Names*. Washington, D.C.: Government Printing Office.

Osgood, Cornelius. 1971. *The Han Indians: A Compilation of Ethnographic and Historical Data on the Alaska-Yukon Boundary Area*. Yale University Publications in Anthropology, no. 74. New Haven: Department of Anthropology, Yale University.

Patty, Stanton. 1971. "A Conference with the Tanana Chiefs." *Alaska Journal* 1, no. 2 (Spring): 2–18.

Pelto, Pertti. 1973. *The Snowmobile Revolution: Technology and Social Change in the Arctic*. Menlo Park, CA: Cummings Publishing Company.

Peter, Katherine. 2001. *Khehkwaii Zheh Gwiich'i': Living in the Chief's House*. Fairbanks: Alaska Native Language Center.

Potter, Jean. 1947. *The Flying North*. New York: Ballantine Books, Inc.

Pulu, Tupou. 1975. *Nikolai Reader*. Anchorage: Bilingual Education Department, Alaska State-Operated School System.

Quirk, William. 1974. *Historical Aspects of the Building of the Washington-Alaska Military Cable and Telegraph System with Special Emphasis on the Eagle-Valdez and Goodpaster Telegraph Lines, 1902–1903*. Anchorage: U.S. Department of the Interior, Bureau of Land Management.

Ray, Patrick, and W. Richardson. 1900. "Relief of the destitute in the Yukon region, 1898." *Compilation of Narratives of Exploration in Alaska*. Washington, D.C.: Government Printing Office. 517–560.

Raymond, Charles. 1900. "Reconnaissance of the Yukon River, 1869." *Compilation of Narratives of Exploration in Alaska*. Washington, D.C.: Government Printing Office. 19–41.

Rearden, Jim. 2007. *Sam O. White, Alaskan: Tales of a Legendary Wildlife Agent and Bush Pilot*. Missoula, MT: Pictorial Histories Publishing Company, Inc.

Redding, Robert. N.d. *Chatanika Days, 1930s*. Self-published.

Roman, Walter. 1983. Central Reflections, Then and Now Project Jukebox, Alaska and Polar Regions, Elmer E. Rasmuson Library, University of Alaska Fairbanks. H87-74-08. http://jukebox.uaf.edu/central/biohtm/warob.html.

Ryden, Ken. 1993. *Mapping the Invisible Landscape: Folklore, Writing, and the Sense of Place*. Iowa City: University of Iowa Press.

Salisbury, Gay, and Laney Salisbury. 2003. *The Cruelest Miles*. New York: W.W. Norton Company.

Schneider, William. N.d. "An Alaskan Success: Career Soldier Patrick Henry Ray." In possession of author.

————. 1976. "Beaver, Alaska: The Story of a Multi-ethnic Community." Ph.D. dissertation. Bryn Mawr College.

————. 1985. "Chief Sesui and Lieutenant Herron: A Story of Who Controls the Bacon." *Alaska History* 1, no. 2: 1–18.

————. 1986. "On the Back Slough: Ethnohistory of Interior Alaska." *Interior Alaska: A Journey through Time*. Robert Thorson. Anchorage: Alaska Geographic Society. 147–194.

Schwantes, Carlos. 2003. *Going Places: Transportation Redefines the Twentieth-Century West*. Bloomington: Indiana University Press.

Schwatka, Frederick. 1900. "A Reconnaissance of the Yukon Valley, 1883." *Compilation of Narratives of Explorations in Alaska*. Washington, D.C.: Government Printing Office. 285–362.

Scott, Elva. 1997. *Jewel on the Yukon, Eagle City: Collection of Essays on Historic Eagle and Its People*. Eagle, AK: Eagle Historical Society & Museums.

Sheppard, William. 2004. "The Significance of Dog Traction for the Analysis of Prehistoric Societies." *Alaska Journal of Anthropology* 1–2: 70–82.

Sherwood, Morgan. 1965. *Exploration of Alaska, 1865–1902*. New Haven: Yale University Press.

Simpson, Sherry. 1996. "Heroes of the Mail Trail." *Alaska Magazine* 62 (February): 20–25.

Skilbred, John. 1998. *Charlie Biederman: Legend of the Mail Trail*. Americopy Publishing.

Snider, Irving. 1939. Film #16-3, Reel 3, chapter 3, Percy DeWolfe leaves with mail for Eagle Alaska. Yukon Archives, Irving Snider fonds, 86/98, Snider Film 3, 16 mm, V-44-3.

Stirling, Dale. 1982. *An Overview of Aviation History in Alaska with an Emphasis on Float and Ski Plane Use*. Anchorage: Policy Research and Land Entitlement, Division of Research and Development, Department of Natural Resources, State of Alaska. 1–15.

Stout, Al. 1991. Yukon-Charley Rivers National Preserve Project Jukebox.

Stroecker, E. H. 1947. Oral history interview for KFAR radio, "Here's a Pioneer." Oral History Collection, Rasmuson Library, H75-08.

Stuck, Hudson. 2005 [1914]. *Ten Thousand Miles with a Dog Sled: A Narrative of Winter Travel in Interior Alaska*. Rye Brook, NY: Adamant Media.

Tidd, Clauide Bretiff. N.d. "Glimpses of Life in the Yukon: 100,000 Miles with a Dog Team." MSS61, 77/19. File 2 of 2, Yukon Archives.

Tordoff, Dirk. 2002. *Mercy Pilot: The Joe Crosson Story*. Kenmore, WA: Epicenter Press.

Ulen, Tishu. 1991. April 29, 1992. Gates of the Arctic Jukebox Program Sec. 1 Oral History Collection 91-22-23. http://jukebox.uaf.edu/gatesN/html/H91-22-32.htm.

Up the Koyukuk. 1983. *Alaska Geographic* 10, no. 4: 46.

U.S. Centennial of Flight Commission. 1925. http://www.CentennialofFlight.gov/essay/Government_Role/1925-29_airmail/POL5.htm.

U.S. Department of Agriculture. 1901. *Fourth Report on the Agricultural Investigations in Alaska*. Office of the Experiment Stations, Director A.C. True. Bulletin no. 94. Georgeson, C.C. Washington, D.C.: Government Printing Office.

U.S. Department of War. 1905. *Annual Report of the War Department for the Fiscal Year Ending June 30, 1905*. Vol. 1: 299–315. Washington, D.C.: Government Printing Office.

———. 1908. *Annual Report*, vol. 1. Washington, D.C.: Government Printing Office.

U.S. Post Office. 1898. *Annual Report of the Post Office Department for 1898, the fiscal year ended June 30, 1898*. Report of the Postmaster General. Miscellaneous Reports. Washington, D.C.: Government Printing Office.

———. 1902. *Report ending 1902, Annual Report of the U.S. Post Office Department for the Fiscal Year Ended June, 1902*. 57th Congress, 2d sess., Doc. 4, House of Representatives. Washington, D.C.: Government Printing Office.

Valdez News. 1901. "Fastest Mail from Circle: Record Broken over 'All American Route'." March 16, pp. 1, 4. (Rex Fisher collection.)

VanStone, James W. 1979. *Ingalik Contact Ecology: An Ethnohistory of the Lower-Middle Yukon, 1790–1935*. Chicago: Field Museum of Natural History. Vol. 71.

———. 1984. "Exploration and Contact History of Western Alaska." Pp. 149–160 in *Handbook of North American Indians: vol. 5, Arctic*. Edited by David Damas. Washington, D.C.: Smithsonian Institution.

Walker, Tom. 2005. *Kantishna: Miners, Mushers, and Mountaineers: The Story Behind Mt. McKinley National Park*. Missoula, MT: Pictorial Histories Publishing Company.

Warren, Frank, and George O'Leary. 2008. Oral history interview by Frank Warren and George O'Leary with William Schneider (interviewer). Oral History Collection, Rasmuson Library, H2008-01.

Warren, Mary. 1994. Central Reflections, Then and Now Project Jukebox, OHC, H95-09-01 and H95-09-02. http://jukebox.uaf.edu/central/biohtm/mawab.html.

Waugaman, Candy. 2007. "Interior Scrapbook." *Fairbanks Daily News-Miner*, December 16, p. E7.

Webb, Melody. 1976. Interview with Horace Biederman. September 18. National Park Service files.

———. 1977. Interview with Charlie Biederman. February 1977. National Park Service files.

———. 1983. "Yukon Frontiers: The Westward Movement to the North Country." PhD dissertation. Albuquerque: University of New Mexico.

———. 1985. *The Last Frontier*. Albuquerque: University of New Mexico Press.

Wickersham, James. 2009. *Old Yukon: Tales, Trails, and Trials*. Fairbanks: University of Alaska Press.

Williams, Jane. 1995. Central Reflections, Then and Now Project Jukebox, OHC, H95-21. http://jukebox.uaf.edu/central/biohtm/jawib.html.

Williams, William. 1992. Gates of the Arctic Project Jukebox, OHC, H93-15-15.
    http://jukebox.uaf.edu/GatesN/allakak/wiwi.htm.
Wilson, William. 1977. *Railroad in the Clouds: The Alaska Railroad in the Age of
    Steam, 1914–1945*. Boulder, CO: Pruett Publishing Co.
Woodall, R. G. 1976. *The Postal History of Yukon Territory, Canada*. Laurence, MA:
    Quarterman Publications.
Woods, Harold, and Richard Frank. 1987. Oral history interview with Pete
    Bowers and William Schneider. OHC, H87-30.
Yarber, Yvonne, and Curt Madison. 1985. *Stanley Dayo: A Biography*. For Yukon-
    Koyukuk School District. Fairbanks: Spirit Mountain Press.

Index